The covenant is such a rich and powerful truth in the Bible, and yet so few people really understand its power and meaning. In her book, Heather Wilson helps to provide clarity and understanding in a clear, practical, and personal way. Heather writes from her own experience, having a deep and abiding love relationship with the Lord Jesus. She has been driven by the power of the Covenant initiated by her Lord. As she has lived out this relationship on a daily basis, she has gleaned much, and in her book she shares those exciting and life-giving lessons with us. It is a "great read" and I heartily recommend it to you!

Eric Hystad, Associate Pastor of Second Baptist Church of Houston, Texas

Blessings *of a* Covenant God

Heather Lynn Wilson

CROSSBOOKS
PUBLISHING

CrossBooks™
A Division of LifeWay
1663 Liberty Drive
Bloomington, IN 47403
www.crossbooks.com
Phone: 1-866-879-0502

First published by CrossBooks 12/28/2012

ISBN: 978-1-4627-2352-2 (sc)
ISBN: 978-1-4627-2351-5 (hc)
ISBN: 978-1-4627-2353-9 (e)

Library of Congress Control Number: 2012922305

Printed in the United States of America

This book is printed on acid-free paper.

CONTENTS

This book is dedicated to my Husband, Dean who always believed in me.

INTRODUCTION

Walking through the streets of the quaint town of Haleiwa, Hawaii, in search an artist who, my husband said, painted glowing fish, we found ourselves visiting just about every art gallery in this laid-back surfer's paradise. We were determined to buy a painting representing one of our favorite towns in the islands. Haleiwa mainly consisted of surf shops and art galleries, but each unique, historic plantation building told a story of its own. Located on the North Shore of Oahu, Haleiwa is a surfer's dream because of the famous beaches of Waimea Bay including Banzai Pipeline and Sunset Beach.

Our search produced no glowing fish. We sat awhile on a park bench, enjoying the town's ambiance, and when I looked up, I saw a rainbow. Most of the time, you see only half a rainbow or bits and pieces while the end is lost in the clouds. This time, however, I beheld the full arc. My eyes followed the glowing arc from the beginning to the end, and I realized that it was a double rainbow! I had never seen such a thing. I couldn't help but smile.

We decided to head toward Sunset Beach to watch the surfers and catch the sunset. Along the way, we noticed a small house with surfboards sitting in the front yard like gravestones. Most of them were cut in half, and some were full-length boards, but all were painted with a beautiful beach picture. Intrigued, we walked up to the house to get a closer look. The surfboards were painted with beautiful bright pink, orange, and purple sunsets, crisp, blue-green breaking waves, and white, sandy beaches.

As we admired the artwork, one of the artists came out to introduce himself. His name was Ron, he said, and he painted retired surfboards for a living. Surfers whose boards were broken or damaged gave them to him. All the locals knew was that he cleaned them up and used each one to paint a scenic portrait of a piece of Haleiwa. We told him we were newlyweds and were looking for a piece of artwork as a remembrance of our trip.

"Then you've come to the right place!" Ron said.

I studied each board intently, wondering what these things might cost. I really wanted to find one with a rainbow on it like the one I had just seen.

The rainbow is the sign God gave to man to represent His promise never to flood the earth again. In the Bible, rainbows symbolize God's covenant with every human being and every living creature on earth. "I have set my rainbow in the clouds, and it will be the sign of the covenant between me and the earth," He says in Genesis 9:13 NIV.

Married less than twenty-four hours, I had just entered into a covenant with God and my husband, vowing to God that I would dedicate the rest of my life to my husband. To me, the rainbow was God's beautiful reminder of His ultimate protection and His vow that He will always keep His promises. The rainbow is a sign of God's faithfulness, and I desperately wanted to find a board that had one on it.

Ron asked me if anything appealed to me, and I said, "I'm looking for one with a rainbow."

"Oh, a sign of God's covenant with man," he said.

I was dumbfounded that he had read my mind. His response opened the door to deeper conversation for the rest of the day.

Ron led me to a half-board on which he had painted a picture of a Haleiwa wave with a rainbow hovering over it. He began to explain the uniqueness of the waves that drew surfers to the North Shore. The variety of waves makes the Banzai Pipeline's reef break unique. Researching the Pipeline, I found that it is notorious for massive waves that break right above closely spaced reefs. This causes the waves to have a tube-like effect, which allows a surfer to glide through it. In addition, the Pipeline has three reefs further out in the ocean that produce four infamous waves that the surfer can ride. Depending on the swell direction or the way the wave breaks at its peak, it can curl off to the left or barrel off to the right.

As I thought about what Ron was saying, I realized these waves—which surfers come from all over the world to ride— represented all the choices we have in life. Atop the wave's peak, you have the option to surf it left or right.

Isaiah 30:21NIV tells us, "Whether you turn to the right or to the left, your ears will hear a voice behind you, saying, 'This is the way; walk in it.'" The way is pointed out to us, but we always have a choice. However, as long as we are living under the rainbow, within God's covenant, His voice will always be there saying, "Follow me."

Scripture tells us that it takes a lifetime to build a reputation and a second to lose it. We are free moral agents with the ability to choose. As we surf the wave of life, we have the choice to go to the right or to the left. That choice will always be in front of us, and the rainbow will always be above us. All we have to do is look up to know without a doubt that God's promises will never fail.

As we study the Bible, we see God initiating covenants with man. We may doubt ourselves, but we need not doubt the faithfulness of God. Scripture tells us that God is compassionate, gracious, slow to anger, abounding in love and faithfulness. We may not be able to trust that we will always make the right decisions in life, but we can trust in the character of God.

Part of God's character is how He chooses to interact with humanity. We see that the principle of covenant is used to describe the relationship between God and humanity in the Old and the New Testaments. We don't see man negotiating with God but God making covenants with man. How reassuring to know that our Lord and Savior is a rock for His people. There is a beauty in the word *covenant*. It is pure, trustworthy, reliable, and forever—because it represents whom God is.

chapter 1

A LOVE THAT BINDS

> I will make a covenant of peace with them; it will be an everlasting covenant. I will establish them and increase their numbers, and I will put my sanctuary among them forever. My dwelling place will be with them; I will be their God, and they will be my people. Then the nations will know that I the Lord make Israel holy, when my sanctuary is among them forever.
>
> —Ezek. 37:26–28 NIV

When I was a little girl, I dreaded each trip to the dentist. I remember lying back in the big, cold chair, hearing the metal tools scrape against my teeth. I would hold my breath and try to imagine I was somewhere else. This phobia still plagues me today, even though I've never had a cavity.

My childhood dentist tried to make the experience as much fun as possible for patients like me by placing crazy pictures on the walls. The pictures were called autostereograms. An autostereogram is a picture inside another picture. It is designed to create the optical illusion of a three-dimensional scene from a two-dimensional image. To understand the picture, you have to overcome its natural appearance by focusing intently. *What a smart idea,* I thought—staring into the depths of an optical illusion to take one's mind off of what was really going on. When viewed with proper intensity, the repeating patterns appear to float above or below the background. Some people see the true picture right away; others stare and stare and it never comes to them. I would always squint my eyes and stare as hard as I could until it finally came to me.

When God put a burden on my heart to write about covenants, I thought that the word *covenant* was an ancient Old Testament word, but it's not. In *Expository Dictionary of Bible Words,* Larry Richards writes,

> The notion of a covenant is unfamiliar today. But the concept of covenant is utterly basic to our understanding of Scripture. In Old Testament times this complex concept was the foundation of social order and social relations, and it was particularly the foundation for an understanding of humanity's relationship with God.[1]

I also thought of the Old Testament as an autostereogram or picture I just didn't get. I have read and re-read the Old Testament and still I put my Bible down and wonder what all the rituals, ceremonies, names, and places really mean. Knowing that God is not a God of confusion but a God of order, purpose, and significance, we can be sure there is divine purpose behind every word of Scripture. Someone

[1]   Larry Richards, *Expository Dictionary of Bible Words* (Grand Rapids, MI: Zondervan, 1985).

once told me that there is a picture of Jesus Christ in every Old Testament story. The Old Testament paints a picture of the Good News—the Gospel—and a picture of God the Father, Jesus, and the Holy Spirit. Jesus Himself confirmed that the entire Old Testament points to His blood covenant with humanity (Luke 24:25–27).

When you think about it, the Old Testament really is an autostereogram, or a picture within a picture. Covenants in the Old Testament were always sealed in blood. People would enter into a relationship and sign the deal in blood, so to speak. This blood came from animal sacrifices, which foreshadowed the ultimate sacrifice, Jesus Christ. Jesus' blood on Calvary confirmed the new covenant. A holy God reached out to humanity and initiated His plan to cultivate relationships with sinners like you and me. I believe that God created a desire in all of us to establish relationships. We were made to bond with our family and purse friendships. That need also awakens us to our need for God.

This book explores how God reaches out to humanity and discusses the blessings that come from being in a relationship with Him. Together, let us stay a little longer and stare a little harder so that, with the help of the Holy Spirit, we too may eventually understand. This book is not about comparing the Old Testament to the New. It's about recognizing that the God of the universe is reaching out to us and asking us to be a part of something greater than ourselves. It's about seeing the hand of God in everyday life and taking Him at His Word. It's about seeing God throughout the Bible—the Old and New Testaments—and holding on to His promises.

St. Augustine, whom many consider to be one of the most influential figures in the ancient Western church, said this about the Old and New Testaments: "The New is in the Old contained; the Old is by the New explained."[2] By examining the word covenant and its meaning we will draw closer to a living, powerful God. To study the word covenant, and to hold on to the promises that come from being in a relationship with a covenant God, there comes an overwhelming since of grace. Understanding that God is a covenant God can and will enrich us with a peace and security we have not know before. Andrew Murray, the gifted nineteenth-century author of the book *The Two Covenants*, says this about having a relationship with a covenant God:

> Happy is the person who truly knows God as his Covenant God and understands what the Covenant promises him. What an unwavering confidence of expectation it secures, guaranteeing that all its terms will be fulfilled to him! What a claim and hold it gives him on the Covenant-keeping God Himself! To many a person, who has never thought much of the Covenant, a true and living faith in it would mean the transformation of his whole life. The full knowledge of what God wants to do for him and the assurance He will certainly do it makes the Covenant the very gate of heaven. May the Holy Spirit give us insight into some of its glory.[3]

---

2   St. Augustine of Hippo, "Types and Anti-types," Dispensational Truths, Clarence Larkin, Blue Letter Bible, http://www.blueletterbible.org/larkin/dt/28.cfm (accessed June 28, 2012).

3   Andrew Murray, *The Two Covenants* (Ft. Washington, Pennsylvania 19034: CLC Publications, 2005), Pages 15-16.

What a Covenant Is

If you look up the word *covenant* in a Bible dictionary, you will see it defined as a promise or a binding agreement. *Holman's Bible Dictionary* defines a covenant as an "oath-bound promise whereby one party solemnly pledges to bless or serve another party in some specified way."[4]

Sometimes keeping the promise depends on meeting certain conditions by the party to whom the promise is made. On other occasions, the promise is made unilaterally or unconditionally. Today you don't hear the word covenant used much to describe the character of God. But as I studied the word covenant I reached a since of security that I had never experienced with any human being. I felt a peace that calmed my natural ability to want to prove myself and I experienced a since of gratitude towards God that overwhelmed my heart.

In *Our Covenant God*, Kay Arthur writes,

> By the grace of God's Spirit (you will) experience … a security you have never known, as you realize that everything God does is based on covenant. Your discoveries will unlock a very old truth—a truth once understood, valued, and lived by in the Semitic world of the Bible. It is a truth that will forever change your understanding of God and what it means to be His child.

She adds this:

> Once you understand and embrace the reality that God is a God of covenant, you will

---

[4] Holman Illustrated Bible Dictionary, s.v. "Covenant."

experience a peace, strength, a security you have never known. The Word of God will take on a whole new dimension, delighting you with wonder as you explore the height, the depth, the breadth of what it means to be in covenant with God. The words *lovingkindness* and *friend* will take on new meaning and become so precious as you identify them as covenant terms. You will never read the Bible the same way again. For covenant takes the veil off the truth.

Freedom from bondage will come, as you comprehend-from the perspective of covenant-the relationship of law to grace. Peace will invade your soul, opening the gate into His pleasant green pastures of rest as you explore the everlasting love that keeps and guards you—and never abandons you.[5]

What a Covenant Is Not

We must not look at a covenant as a contract. Even though both draw two parties together, a covenant and a contract are not the same. Of course we can relate to a contract, a binding agreement between two parties. At some point in our lives, we all have signed our names to contracts of some sort. I signed my first contract when I bought my first home. At first I thought I could represent myself and save money by not hiring a real-estate agent. I learned quickly that I needed an

---

5   Kay Arthur, *Our Covenant God* (Colorado Springs, Colorado 80921: Waterbrook Press, 1999), Pages 15-16.

agent to explain what I was binding myself to by agreeing to sign on the dotted line. God's covenant, by contrast, doesn't have loopholes or fine print.

There are no "gotchas" or "traps" that we later discover we overlooked. We can view God's covenant as an act of love—a love that always has our best interests at heart. The Bible says that God is love (1John 4:8 NIV). After studying the meaning of covenant, I realized that all of God's interactions with humanity are based on covenant, an act of His love. His covenant with us binds us forever to Him eternally. Charles H. Spurgeon views the word covenant as:

The Covenant is …
A treasury of wealth,
A granary of food,
A fountain of life,
A storehouse of salvation,
A charter of peace
And a haven of joy.[6]

God is a covenant God. This is how He operates. God's initiation of covenants with His people is a theme throughout Scripture. Come with me as we explore this characteristic of God.

Holy Father, give us understanding of who You are. Help us know Your faithfulness to Your people. Thank You that Your Word says we are rooted and established in Your love. I pray for all the saints reading this book, asking that You would help us grasp how wide and how long and high and deep the love of Christ is for us. For we

6   Charles H Spurgeon "The Messenger of the Covenant," Phillip R. Johnson, http://www.spurgeon.org/sermons/0470.htm (accessed June 7, 2012).

know that this love, surpassing our knowledge,
will fill us to the measure of all the fullness of God.
In Jesus' name we pray.

God Initiates

Then the Lord told Abram, "Leave your country,
your relatives, and your Father's house, and go
to the land that I will show you."

—Gen. 12:1 NLT

For something to have significance with God, God must
initiate it.

I was single and living in a one-bedroom apartment in Houston's Galleria area. I loved my little apartment, my friends, my church, and the church family God had given me. I was serving in our high school ministry department as I had done for eight years, and I was happy.

However, God began to stir in me the feeling that it was time for a change. He put a burden on my heart to pack up and move though I didn't know where or why. Every time I opened my Bible, I was given Genesis 12:1, the story about how God told Abraham to pack up his family and move. Abraham didn't know where, but God said He would show him. My lease was up, and I had to sign for another six months, thinking it would take about that long to find a new place to live.

I began to pray, asking God whether He wanted me to lease or to buy a house. I had never owned a home before but was intrigued by the thought. If God wanted me to buy, then I had confidence He would provide.

As I began my search, God put a burden on my heart to move to Pearland, Texas. There I felt God directing my path. I would view homes with my realtor, and Christian music would be playing on the radio. I would meet a group of ladies at a coffee shop, and they would invite me to be a part of their Bible study. As I sought the Lord, God was telling me that this place was my rest—this was where I was to move. I found a house in my price range and got my finances together.

Things were falling into place, and I knew that it was not a coincidence; it was God's doing.

This all happened within a month. The only problem was that I still had a six-month lease with the apartment complex. I knew there would probably be a financial obligation to break the lease. My realtor was a Christian and we said a prayer before I called my apartment manager to ask to get out of the lease. As you know, God controls the heart. The manager agreed to allow me out of the lease with no financial obligation.

A new chapter in my life was about to begin. I didn't know what was to come, but I knew I was in God's will. The best feeling in the world is when you know you are right with God and obedient to His calling.

I have learned that the most dramatic changes in my life have come from God's initiative, not my own. The people whom God used mightily in Scripture were all ordinary men and women acting on divine assignments that they never could have initiated or accomplished on their own.

Sometimes we push and push on doors that are never meant to open, and we are miserable because of it. But when God opens doors and tells us to go, then we must go. It may not make sense; it may not feel right. But if it is of God, then we must go.

At times we must put our emotions aside when they disagree with what God is telling us to do. I didn't want to leave my comfortable life in the city and move to a suburban area where I knew no one. But when God moves in our lives, we must move with Him. He is a good God, who has a plan for our lives. "For I know the plans I have for you," declares the Lord, "plans to prosper you and not to harm you, plans to give you hope and a future" (Jer. 29:11 NIV).

Only He knows that plan. I don't want to miss out on the blessings that come from following Jesus. He said we must deny ourselves, pick up our crosses, and follow Him. Imagine what we miss if we don't move when God initiates!

Someone once told me that God is more concerned about timing than time. When He was ready to build a nation for His purposes, the Lord spoke to Abraham and told him to pack up everything and move. God was telling Abraham to leave his comfort zone. And because Abraham was obedient through this nation, Jesus, the Savior of the world, was born. What if Abraham had said, "No, Lord, I'm going to stay right here; I'm comfortable here, I'm happy here, and I deserve to be here"? I believe everything would have worked out the same, but Abraham would have missed out on experiencing what it is like to have nothing to depend upon but God.

God appeared to Moses in the burning bush when it was time to deliver Israel from slavery in Egypt. God wanted to use

Moses to deliver His people. God gave Moses his assignment, and Moses told God that he wasn't capable because he stuttered. Can you imagine that? The God of the universe approaches you, tells you His plan, and invites you to be part of it, and you say, "Well, God, have you heard me speak lately? Why don't you send my brother Aaron instead of me?" God told Moses that He would not only be with him, but He would tell him what to say and how to say it.

An angel of the Lord told Mary she would become pregnant with Jesus, who would be the long-awaited Messiah. "I am the Lord's servant," Mary answered. "May it be to me as you have said" (Luke 1:38 NIV).

When God called, a young, pregnant teenager, who knew that the penalty for what looked to be adultery was death, she answered, "Yes, Lord!"

In God's timing, Jesus selected twelve ordinary, uneducated men and asked them to quit their day jobs, leave their families, and follow Him. These men would be a part of something so great that their lives would never be the same.
We can choose to answer the call of God on our lives like the twelve disciples or be like the rich young ruler.

> As he was starting out on a trip, a man came running up to Jesus, knelt down, and asked, "Good Teacher, what should I do to get eternal life?"
> "Why do you call me good?" Jesus asked. "Only God is truly good. But as for your question, you know the commandments: 'Do not murder. Do not commit adultery. Do not steal. Do not testify

falsely. Do not cheat. Honor your father and mother.'"

"Teacher," the man replied, "I've obeyed all these commandments since I was a child." Jesus felt genuine love for this man and he looked at him. "You lack only one thing," he told him. "Go sell all you have and give the money to the poor, and you will have treasure in heaven. Then come, follow me." At this, the man's face fell, and he went sadly away because he had many possessions.

—Mark 10:17–22 NLT

There is nothing wrong with having money. It's the love of money that Jesus warns us about. Jesus knew what was in this young man's heart. He saw where his heart's devotion was and asked him to give it up. And the man said no.

Jesus can see what is in our hearts and what we esteem higher than Him. The ruler's possessions meant more to him than following the call of God for his life. He was young, rich; well respected in his community, and lived a moral life. But God called him to join Him and His followers. The young man chose his possessions. Sometimes God's call is loud and clear, and then sometimes it is a whisper. Either way He initiates in constantly calling us to follow Him. Can you hear Him calling you now?

God initiates new things, new chapters, new seasons, new events, new relationships, new beginnings in the lives of His people, allowing them to accomplish things that they would never be able to accomplish on their own. Is the Lord initiating something new in your life? What is the Lord calling you to? Are you ready for something new? Join Him in the journey He has for you.

Now to him who is able to do immeasurably more than all we ask or imagine, according to his power that is at work within us, to him be the glory in the church and in Christ Jesus throughout all generations, for ever and ever! Amen.

—Eph. 3:20 ASV

Whom Do You Love to Please?

Am I now trying to win the approval of men, or of God? Or am I trying to please men? If I were still trying to please men, I would not be a servant of Christ.

—Gal. 1:10 ESV

I loved my house in Pearland. I was scared and lonely, but God had provided and I knew He had a plan. My friends, family, and co-workers did not agree with my decision to move. Why would a single girl move to the suburbs, drive further to work, and be further from friends and family and her church home? To be honest, I didn't understand at the time, either.

My whole life I have struggled with pleasing people. I hate confrontation, and God has been working on me about that. To know that others didn't approve of my decisions wore on me, and I would often doubt myself. So, because I had been called a "people pleaser," I had to remind myself that it was God who had initiated and provided this home for me. Because I love to please, I'm the one who eats what I'm given when the waiter messes up my order. But God has taught me that there is a difference between being a peacekeeper and a peacemaker. Those of us who feel it is our responsibility to make everyone happy and contented all the time need to look at what Scripture says about being a peacemaker. Jesus says, "Blessed are the peacemakers, for they will be called sons of God" (Matt. 5:9 NIV).

All of us are called by God to be peacemakers, but we cannot keep the peace for everyone all the time. We are called to make peace between God and man, but we are also called to a righteous anger, an anger that compels us to action. Following God's call will not always be peaceful.

There will be times when we face a choice whether to please God or to please man. It is very important to strive for peace and harmony in our relationships, but not if it causes us to disobey God. Our obedience to God must always take precedence over the opinions of others.

Jesus warned that obeying God could even cause division within our families, among those we value the most.

> Do not suppose that I have come to bring peace to the earth. I did not come to bring peace, but a sword. For I have come to turn a man against his father, a daughter against her mother, a daughter-in-law against her mother-in-law. And a man's enemies will be the members of his own household.
> —Matt. 10:34–36 NIV

It may sound harsh, but there will be times when we may risk losing those close to us because of our relationship with Jesus Christ. In Luke 8:21, Jesus identified His real family as those who hear God's Word and put it into practice. As members of God's family, we may risk hurting others or making them angry. It may look as if we don't value their opinions. Yet, as Christians, we know in our hearts what God has called us to do. We must not allow the opinions of others to dictate our actions.

A Bond Servant of Jesus Christ

Paul said in Galatians 1:10 that if he wasn't obedient to God's call, he could not consider himself a servant of Jesus Christ. The New American Standard Version of the Bible calls such a person a bond-servant, which could be translated as *servant of God* or *God's slave*. The difference between a servant and a slave is that the servant could be paid but the slave is owned. *Bond-servant* is a compound word. The word *bond* means a force that binds or ties together, a solemn promise or pledge or covenant. A bond-servant in the Bible is the one who initiates the bond.

In the New Testament, a Greek word for *servant* is *douls,* which means literally or figuratively, involuntarily or voluntarily willing to serve. Yet when we put the word *bond* in front of the word *servant,* it takes on a different meaning. What does it mean to be a bond-servant of Jesus Christ?

In the Old Testament, having a servant or a slave was common practice. When a Jew found himself in dire poverty, unable to pay his mortgage and feed his family, he could turn to his fellow Jew and sell himself and his family to redeem his property. God set forth rules for how masters were to treat these servants.

> When you buy a Hebrew slave, he shall serve six years, in the seventh he shall go out free, for

> nothing. If he comes in single, he shall go out single; if he comes in married, then his wife shall go out with him. If his master gives him a wife and she bears him sons or daughters, the wife and her children shall be her master's, and he shall go out alone. But if the slave plainly says, 'I love my master, my wife, and my children; I will not go out free,' then his master shall bring him to God, and he shall bring him to the door or the doorpost. And his master shall bore his ear through with an awl, and he shall be his slave forever.
>
> —Ex. 21:2-6 ESV

Masters were called to treat their servants with respect; they could not abuse or mistreat them.

> If your brother becomes poor beside you and sells himself to you, you shall not make him serve as a slave: he shall be with you as a hired servant and as a sojourner. He shall serve with you until the year of jubilee. Then he shall go out from you, he and his children with him, and go back to his own clan and return to the possession of his fathers. For they are my servants, whom I brought out of the land of Egypt; they shall not be sold as slaves. You shall not rule over him ruthlessly but shall fear your God.
>
> —Lev. 25:39–43 ESV

In verse 39, *brother* refers to a fellow Israelite, so the Israelites called by God were not to treat their fellow Israelites like slaves. God reiterated that they were His own people for whom He had made provision. At the end of the sixth year, the servant had a choice to leave and start a new life of his own or stay with his master. If the servant had developed a strong bond with his master, he could choose to remain with him permanently.

The choice to stay or go was in direct correlation to the respect and love the slave had developed for his master. Clearly, if he chose to stay, the servant had been treated with dignity and respect and had developed a strong love for his master and his master's family. The servant was not committing to his master for another six years but to faithfully obey and serve for the rest of his life. By choosing to stay, the servant was making a life-long commitment to surrender himself and his family physically and emotionally into the hands of another. His life would no longer be his own but would be relinquished to his master. He would be committing to his master's plan for his life and for his family's life. He would be living each day in good faith that he would be taken care of for the rest of his life.

According to Scripture, this commitment was to be made publicly. The elders would be witnesses to the covenant made between the servant and his master. The servant would be brought to the door, and his master would bore a hole in his ear with an awl. An awl is a sharp instrument used to pierce the skin. The hole was the lasting mark of servitude. It implied, "I don't belong to myself anymore, and the decision is irreversible." The servant was forever marked as a bond-servant.

The Hebrews viewed the ear as symbolic of obedience. In Scripture, Jesus often says, "He who has ears let him hear." The servant's pierced ear represented his responsiveness to his master's call and willingness to follow it. The ceremony also represented the master's adoption of the servant and his family. Some commentators interpret the servant serving until jubilee, held every fifty years, but this could also be interpreted as forever. We discover in the New Testament that Paul, Peter, and James called themselves bond-servants of Christ or viewed themselves that way.

God's Call

I, the Lord, have called you in righteousness; I will take hold of your hand. I will keep you and will make you to be a covenant for the people and a light for the Gentiles, to open the eyes that are blind, to free captives from prison and to release from the dungeon those who sit in darkness.

—Isa. 42:6–7 NIV

I had been living in Pearland for ten months. I took the ladies I met in the coffee shop up on their offer to join their Bible study, and it provided me companionship and comfort. After months of wondering about my purpose in Pearland, finally it made sense. I began to phase out of high school ministry at my church and attended only on Sundays. The youth minister was just given the daunting task of being the campus pastor for our satellite churches around Houston, and Pearland would be the first to open. The Pearland satellite church would be only three miles from my house!

Because of our ties, the youth minister asked me to help teach an adult Bible study. I said yes, confident that it was part of God's plan. I had taught high school students but not adults, which scared me. As I sought the Lord, He gave me Isaiah

42:6–7. I believe all of us are called to use our spiritual gifts to build up the body of the church. Whenever God calls us to serve Him in a new and different way, to change jobs, to go where we have never been before, we initially experience the fear that comes with change. But God's Word tells us how to deal with our human fear.

"For God did not give us a spirit of timidity, but a spirit of power, of love, and self-discipline" (2 Tim. 1:7 NIV).

Most fear is of the unknown. Fear can be the root of stress in our lives. Research shows that fear triggers more than fourteen hundred known physical and chemical responses and activates more than thirty hormones and neurotransmitters in our brains.

I can remember going night fishing with my grandfather. We didn't have a boat, but he had plenty of friends who did. We would spend our early mornings with his boating friends bass fishing, and in the evening, we would find a pier and hold up a light. One evening my grandfather brought our rubber boots to the pier and said we would wade in the water so we could cast out to a certain point where he knew the bass would be. I looked into the river and couldn't see a thing. It was dark. I could hear the water crashing on the side of the pier. I thought about snakes and alligators and everything else that hunts at night. Grandfather grabbed my hand and said, "Follow me." He held a big, bright light in front of us and told me that as long as I held his hand and followed the light I'd be okay. I trusted him completely and did as he said.

When we venture into the unknown, there will always be fear, but we must remember whom we are following. It may look dark, but Jesus said, "I am the light of the world; he who follows Me shall not walk in darkness but have the light of life" (John 8:12 NIV). As we follow Jesus in a dark world, our fear will be met with divine assurance of His love for us. He knows the way.

When God first approached Abraham, He said in a vision, "Do not be afraid, Abram. I am your shield, your very great reward" (Gen. 15:1 NIV). How comforting these words must have been!

Obviously a great fear must have come over Abraham when he saw the Lord in this dream. Do you see the divine reassurance in God telling him, "I am with you; I will be your shield; I will protect you, and I will be your great reward"? "Abraham," He is saying, "You will be rewarded for your obedience."
As a believer, we are always a witness, either a good one or a bad one, but we are always one. God wants his people to shine His light into dark places. But we cannot shine the light if we are not following the light. In fact, if we are truly following the light then we won't have to shine the light because God's light will shine through us.

In the words of Isaiah 42:6–7 some believe that Isaiah was foreshadowing Jesus Christ. Some believe Isaiah was calling Israel, God's people to serve Him. Nevertheless there is a calling in Isaiah's words and wherever there is a calling there is always a choice. Where has God called you to be a light to the Gentiles, to open eyes that are blind, to free captives from prison, and to release from dungeon those who sit in darkness? You may be the only Bible some people will ever read. How is your print? Is it big enough for others to see at a distance? Or do others have to get really close to read because the letters are so small? If the truth is in you and in me then God will want to use you to set others free.

Covenant in the Old Testament

Abram had recently left Ur of the Chaldeans, his home country, to follow God's call. Venturing out from his native land, from everything that was comfortable, secure, and known into the unknown was, I'm sure, scary for him. Scripture tells us that because Abram believed the Lord, God credited it to him as righteousness.

God promised Abram a blessing. He told Abram to leave his country, his friends, and his family and "go to a place that I will show you." God said that He would make of Abram a great nation. That He would make his name great and bless him, and that because of this he would be a blessing to generations to come. Of course this was hard for Abram to believe, since he was one hundred years old, his wife Sarai was ninety, and they had no children.

In following God's call for our lives, we must realize that the blessings He bestows on us are not just for us. It's amazing that God can do whatever He wants to do, but that by His grace He chooses to use broken, messed-up individuals like you and me to reach a lost world. He allows His blessing to flow through us to others to draw them and us closer to Him.

Abram's response to this promise of blessing was a question to God. He asked God how he would know that God would hold up his end of the deal. How could he be certain that God would come through and bless him this way?

And God responded to Abram by telling him to bring a heifer, a goat, and a ram, each three years of age. Now this may not mean much to you and me, but to Abram it meant everything.

His heart pounded with excitement because he realized that God was about to make a covenant with him. In Abram's day, when God initiated in asking him to sacrifice a heifer, this meant that He was about to make a solemn agreement with Abram.

Today we are so careful not to do any business deal without signing a contract. Unfortunately, we cannot take the risk of trusting someone's word. I'm not saying that we cannot trust God's Word, but when two parties in the Old Testament entered into a covenant, they were performing an act similar to signing a contract.

In the Middle Eastern world, a practice called "making covenant," or "cutting covenant," was common. The Hebrew word for *covenant* is *berth,* meaning *to cut.*

It is hard for us to relate, but the closest comparison we have today to a biblical covenant is a traditional marriage. God designed marriage so that two should become one flesh. There are ten steps to the Old Testament covenant process that are very symbolic of what happens today in a traditional covenant marriage.

In *The Covenant of Marriage,* Dennis Rainey writes the following:

> In the Old Testament days a covenant was solemn and binding. When the two people entered into a covenant with one another, a goat or lamb would be slain and its carcass would be cut in half. With the two halves separated and lying on the ground, the two people who had formed

the covenant would solemnize their promise by walking between the two halves saying, 'May God do so to me (cut me in half) if I ever break this covenant with you and God!' You get the feeling that a covenant in those days had just a little more substance than today.[7]

The covenant-making process in biblical times was a serious act. People were putting their lives on the line for each other.

Step one of the covenant-making process was the exchanging of robes. Exchanging robes represented an exchange of identities. The two parties entering into a covenant would exchange their outer garments.

I have a fraternal twin sister. We looked more alike when we were younger. Sometimes we would switch clothes and try to trick our mother. When she saw us walking toward her at a distance, wearing the other's clothes, she did not know who was who. I have a friend with identical twin girls who look so much alike that she uses nail polish on one of the sisters to identify them. The twins are completely individual, but from a mother's point of view they are both her children. In marriage, we know two become one. Entering into a covenant marriage, we are still individuals, but God also sees us as one. So when we hurt the other person with our words or actions, we are in essences hurting ourselves because we are forever connected to our covenant partner.

---

7   Dennis Rainey, "The Covenant of Marriage," P-R-E-C-E—T A-U-S-T-I-N, http://www.preceptaustin.org/the_covenant_marriage.htm (accessed June 28, 2012).

In marriage, we often see the female taking on a new name and both parties a new identity as husband and wife. When we become Christians, we take on a new identity as children of God. "Therefore, if anyone is in Christ, he is a new creation; the old has gone, the new has come!" (2 Cor. 5:17 NIV)

At the moment of our salvation, every sin we have committed or will commit is forgiven through the blood of Jesus Christ. We are given a new identity in Christ. We are given a new name as a child of God. God adopts us as His children when we receive His Spirit and become one with Him.

> For you did not receive a spirit that makes you a slave again to fear, but you received the Spirit of sonship. And by him we cry, "Abba, Father." The Spirit himself testifies with our spirit that we are God's children. Now if we are children, then we are heirs—heirs of God and co-heirs with Christ, if indeed we share in his sufferings in order that we may also share in his glory.
> —Rom. 8:15–17 NIV

In the second step of the covenant, the two parties would exchange belts to represent an exchange of strength or assets. These belts were far larger than the belts we wear today. In war, men would hang their military equipment on their heavy-duty belts.

When two people become one in marriage, they can strengthen one another in word and in deed. They can share each other's burdens and help carry each other's loads.

Two people can accomplish more than twice as much as one; they get a better return for their labor. If one person falls, the other can reach out and help. But people who are alone when they fall are in real trouble. And on a cold night, two under the same blanket can gain warmth from each other. But how can one be warm alone? A person standing alone can be attacked and defeated, but two can stand back-to-back and conquer. Three are even better, for a triple-braided cord is not easily broken.

—Eccl. 4:9–12 NLT

Of course the third in the triple-braided cord could represent God, since He holds the covenant marriage together. As strength is drawn from the Lord, grace is given to strengthen the marriage.

In the third step of the covenant, the weapons that hung on the individual's belt also were exchanged. The exchange of weapons represented an exchange of enemies. As the two parties became one, they would fight each other's enemies together.

In a covenant marriage, we are called to defend our partner. We are now on the same side, and when one is weak the other can be strong. Our best defensive weapon could be to pray for our partners. By asking our spouses how we can pray for them and then doing so, could be the best line of defense. Sometimes our most significant callings can be right in front of us.

As children of God, we face the world differently. The world is no longer our friend but our enemy. If you have been a Christian long enough, you know how hard it is to fight the allurements of the world. Jesus said that as children of God we are in the world but not of the world. For children of God, the world becomes a battlefield, as do our own flesh and the schemes of the devil. With Christ, we stand on the same side; the side of truth, and the Holy Spirit enables us to claim victory over temptations that come our way.

The fourth covenant step was the sacrifice of an animal or animals, hence a blood covenant. The Old Testament Hebrew word for *covenant* is *berith,* derived from a root that means *to cut.* God had made other covenants with man in the Bible, but the covenant made with Abram could be considered the most significant for believers. The Abrahamic covenant was not only for him but also for all believers, all of Abraham's descendants. God's covenant with Abram was a blood covenant. Remember God's promise to Abram of land and a seed. The seed was Jesus Christ. The covenant God made with Abram promised the Messiah, our Lord and Savior Jesus Christ, for all who believe, and this covenant was sealed in blood.

> The promises were spoken to Abraham and to his seed. Scripture does not say "and to seeds," meaning many people, but "and to your seed," meaning one person, who is Christ. What I mean is this: The law, introduced 430 years later, does not set aside the covenant previously established by God and thus do away with the promise. For if the inheritance depends on the law, then it

no longer depends on a promise; but God in his
grace gave it to Abraham through a promise.
                                        —Gal. 3:16–18 NIV

Abram knew that through this act of cutting a covenant with
God he could trust His promise. Though Abram would not live
to witness the promise come to pass, he knew God's Word
was irrevocable.

In Abram's day, when men would cut a covenant, should the
covenant be broken, both knew that God Himself would deal
with the one who broke it. In fact, a covenant cut in blood, if
broken, would often require the blood of the one who broke
the covenant. Scripture tells us that it is against God's nature to
lie. When the God of the universe gives His Word, it is so. Abram
witnessed God giving His Word, His promise, giving Himself to
those who would choose Him through Jesus Christ. Through
the blood of Christ, we enter into a covenant with God.

I pondered why must blood be shed to cut a covenant?
Leviticus 17:11 NIV tells us, "For the life of the creature is in
the blood, and I have given it to you to make atonement for
yourselves on the altar; it is the blood that makes atonement
for one's life."

Leviticus 19:2 NIV shouts of the holiness of God: "Speak to the
entire assembly of Israel and say to them: 'Be holy because I,
the Lord your God, am holy.'"
But how do unholy people approach a holy God? Leviticus
gives specific instructions for offering sacrifices that pave the
way to a holy God. These sacrifices foreshadow the ultimate
sacrifice that was Jesus Christ.

Charles H. Spurgeon comments on how life rest in the blood,

> Scripture teaches us … that the blood produces life—that life lies in the blood. Blood, therefore, is the mysterious link between matter and spirit. How it is that the soul should in any degree have alliance with matter through blood, we cannot understand; but certain it is that this is the mysterious link which unites these apparently dissimilar things together, so that the soul can inhabit the body, and the life can rest in the blood.[8]

The fact that blood produces life is a well-known medical truth. A creature cannot live without blood flowing through its body. Have you ever seen a sign advertising to give blood? If you have, perhaps you will remember the slogan "Give blood, give life." From a spiritual perspective, the blood of Jesus is what gives eternal life.

In addition, the blood of animals shed in the Old Testament foreshadowed the cost of forgiveness. Without the sacrificial shedding of blood, there is no forgiveness of sins (Heb. 9:22 NIV). God required animal sacrifices to provide a temporary covering of sin. Yet Jesus' ultimate sacrifice of Himself provided the final sacrifice of blood needed to pave the way to God.

When we consider the functions of blood in the human body, we can also view them from a spiritual perspective. There are seven biological functions of human blood.

---

8   Charles H. Spurgeon, "A Call to Holy Living," Phillip R. Johnson, http://www.spurgeon.org/sermons/1029.htm.

1) Blood transports metabolic wastes from each cell to organs that excrete them. Blood cleanses the body. Those covered with the blood of Christ have been cleansed of their sin. Sin no longer reigns over them. What once was a crimson stain now is considered as white as snow in the eyes of God. "God made him who had no sin, to be sin, for us, so that in him we might become the righteousness of God" (2Cor. 5:21 NIV).

2) Red blood cells transport oxygen from the lungs to other cells of the body. When God made Adam, the Bible tells us, he wasn't fully alive until God breathed life into him. The Word says that Scripture is God-breathed, written by man but inspired by God Himself. Nothing becomes alive until God breathes life into it.

3) Blood transports nutrients from the digestive system and from storage depots to each cell of the body. "Then Jesus declared, 'I am the bread of life. Whoever comes to Me will never go hungry, and whoever believes in me will never be thirsty'" (John 6:35 NIV). Our natural human hunger could be a reminder from Jesus of our spiritual hunger for Him.

4) Blood transports hormones from endocrine glands to target tissues. The term *hormone* is derived from a Greek word meaning *to excite*. The blood of Christ stimulates a change in our desires. As Christians, our desires become the desires of God Himself. A desire for holiness overcomes the desire for happiness. What used to excite us now may disgust us. What we used to think would bring us pleasure now brings pain and sorrow. Someone once said that sin will take you further than you wanted to go, make you pay more than you ever wanted to pay, and make you become someone you never wanted to be. When you become a new creature in Christ, your new

life will make you want to live to please God instead of your old sinful nature. Scripture says that if we delight ourselves in the Lord, He will give us the desires of our heart. And thank goodness that our desires change when we become a new creation in Him.

5) Blood helps maintain fluid balance in the body. Have you ever been dehydrated? Losing an excessive amount of water can cause headaches, muscle cramping, and dizziness, even fainting. Balance means a state of equilibrium or equality of distribution.

In its definition of *balance, Vine's Bible Dictionary* refers us to the word *yoke*. A yoke is a curved piece of wood laid on the necks of two oxen, horses, or mules.[9] These animals are bound together by the yoke to keep them in sync with one another as they walk together. When Jesus told us not to be unequally yoked, He was saying we should not bind ourselves to others who are headed in a different spiritual direction.

Jesus said, "Come to Me all you who labor and are heavy laden, and I will give you rest. Take My yoke upon you and learn from Me, for I am gentle and lowly in heart and you will find rest for you souls. For My yoke is easy and my burden is light" (Matt. 11:28—30 ESV). When we are walking with Jesus, we are in sync and in balance. When we are in tune with the Holy Spirit and walking with Jesus, He can carry us through anything.

6) Blood helps distribute metabolic heat within the body and to maintain normal body temperature.

---

9   Vine's Bible Dictionary, s.v. "Balance".

I am miserable when I am cold. I go snow skiing at least once a year, and I've learned many lessons over the years. The most important one is this: it doesn't matter how cutely I dress on the slopes. What matters is whether am I warm. I may have on sock liners, wool socks, glove liners, two pairs of long johns, and two fleece sweatshirts under my ski suit, but at least I'm warm. I may look like the Michelin man, but whatever will keep me from getting to the point of losing all feeling in my hands and feet, and almost crying as I thaw out by the fire, is a good thing. I've been skiing down a slope when it was five below zero and snowing so hard I could not see where I was going. At that point, I knew I'd better get off the mountain and go home. There are times in life when I'm caught in a snowstorm; it's cold, I can't see where I'm going, and I long to get to a warm, safe place. Let the Lord be your refuge in the midst of your storm. "The Lord is a refuge for the oppressed, a stronghold in times of trouble" (Ps. 9:9 NIV).

7) White blood cells defend the body against invading microorganisms. The blood is the body's primary defense against disease and sickness. The blood fights our battles for us. God equips us to fight our battles, too. God's Word is a double-edged sword. It's the only part of the armor given to us to protect ourselves that also is used as a weapon. Jesus always used Scripture to confront the devil when he came against Him. The Lord would say, "For it is written."

> God is our refuge and strength, always ready to help in times of trouble. So we will not fear, even if earthquakes come and the mountains crumble into the sea. Let the oceans roar and foam. Let the mountains tremble as the waters surge! A river brings joy to the city of our God, the sacred

home of the Most High. God himself lives in that city; it cannot be destroyed. God will protect it at the break of day. The nations are in an uproar, and kingdoms crumble! God thunders, and the earth melts! The Lord Almighty is here among us; the God of Israel is our fortress.

—Ps. 46:1–7 NLT

The fifth step in the covenant was the "walk of death." In Genesis 15:10, we see Abram taking a heifer and laying her on her back flat on the ground, with the underside of her belly sliced in two. He takes a goat and a ram, cuts them in half, and lays each half opposite the other. The covenant partners stood facing each other while the animals lay cut open between them. The partners walked between the spilled blood. One would walk through and return on the left side; the other would turn through to the right. Together they formed a figure eight. Here is how God performed this task with Abram:

As the sun went down and it became dark, Abram saw a smoking firepot and a flaming torch pass between the halves of the carcasses. So the Lord made a covenant with Abram that day and said, "I have given this land to your descendants, all the way from the border of Egypt to the great Euphrates River—the land of the Kenites, Kenizzites, Kadmonites, Hittites, Perizzites, Rephaites, Amorites, Canaanites, Girgashites, and Jebusites.

—Gen. 15:17–21 NLT

Fire and smoke in the Bible propose God's holiness and His zeal for righteousness. God took the initiative, gave the confirmation, and followed through on His promise. God's passing through the pieces was a visible assurance to Abram that the covenant God was establishing was real.

A covenant in biblical times was considered a lifelong agreement that could end in death if one went against one's word. After the sacrificial animal's parts were laid opposite one another, the individuals cutting covenant would walk between the parts. This represented the "walk of death," indicating one who broke the covenant would give up his life. In addition, if one were to die before the other, the survivor would uphold the covenant forever. Cutting a covenant was a pledge to uphold it even after death.

God promised Abram a seed from his own body. And God told Abram that through this seed all nations would be blessed. God told Abram to count the stars; if he could count them, he could also number his descendants. It was God who initiated cutting a covenant with Abram. It was God who walked between the pieces, symbolized as "a smoking oven and a flaming torch."

When I think of the marriage covenant and this step of the covenant process, I see how a marriage is to represent to the world the commitment that God makes to us. In marriage, we verbally confess before God, family, and friends that we will never forsake our spouse. We are saying that the covenant we are making before God, family, and friends is irrevocable. We are promising to love through sickness and health, through good and bad times, and even when we don't feel like it. Based on covenant, God has made such a promise to us.

Scripture tells us that God is not a man that he should lie. He is not a human, that he should change his mind. Has he ever spoken and failed to act? Has he ever promised and not carried it through? (Numbers 23:19 NLT). When God makes a promise he keeps it!

In a marriage covenant, two selfish sinners pledge their love to one another for a lifetime. You could view marriage as a "walk of death," knowing that to esteem your partner's needs higher than your own, you first must die to your needs.

I was sitting in a doctor's waiting room watching *The Oprah Winfrey Show* on television across the room. Oprah was interviewing couples about their secrets to a happy marriage. Oprah asked one of the wives about her current husband in contrast with her ex-husband. She boldly proclaimed how wonderful her current husband was, saying he treated her with love and respect and cared for her every need. Oprah was so impressed that she asked the husband how he accomplished all this. He replied that he had learned how to die to himself. Oprah was astounded with his answer. She told the wife, "You've taught him well." The wife replied, "No, God has taught him well."

When one of the guests heard this comment, he said, "Of course he treats his wife well. He's dead! He doesn't have an opinion about anything, so of course you think he's wonderful." My heart broke because this couple was trying to emphasize a godly principle on national television. This so-called secret is no secret at all according to God's blueprint for a biblical marriage. When we crucify the flesh and walk in the Spirit, we will be a delight to others.

When the Holy Spirit controls our lives, He will produce this kind of fruit in us: love, joy, peace, patience, kindness, goodness, faithfulness, gentleness, and self-control. Here there is no conflict with the law. Those who belong to Christ Jesus have nailed the passions and desires of sinful nature to His cross and crucified them there (Gal. 6:22 NIV).

The early twentieth-century Scottish minister Oswald Chambers once said, "No love of the natural heart is safe unless the human heart has been satisfied by God first."[10]

Even when we don't feel like loving our partner, if we choose to do so, God's strength will enable us by the power of the Holy Spirit to esteem others higher than ourselves. Think of the "walk of death" that Jesus Christ performed for you and me. Think how our Lord and Savior died on a cross so you and I could live. Jesus knew His purpose and put aside His emotion for what God called Him to do.

In the Old Testament, over a fifteen-hundred-year period, a veil in the temple separated the people from the Holy of Holies, the place where God dwelled. Only the priests were allowed to go beyond the veil and then just once a year to offer sacrifices for the forgiveness of the people's sins. After Jesus was crucified, the veil was torn from top to bottom, indicating God had made a way through the veil. The tearing of Jesus' flesh in death opened the way to God Almighty. Jesus demonstrated the ultimate walk of death in his walk to the cross on his own initiative.

---

10   Oswald Chambers, *The Best from all His Books Volume II* (Nashville, Tennessee, Thomas Nelson, 1989), Page 184.

The sixth step in the covenant-making ceremony was called the "striking of hands" it represented a mark on the body. In the Hebrew culture, the hand includes the wrist. The covenant partners made incisions in their wrists, put their wrists together, and mingled their blood. When I was a little girl of seven or eight, my best friend and I cut our fingers and mixed our blood together, calling us "blood sisters." We didn't know what we were doing, but we made a vow that we'd be best friends for life. In a traditional Christian marriage a husband and wife will exchange wedding bands to represent an outward appearance on the body of eternity.

Jesus experienced outward scars on his broken body. Nails were driven through Jesus' wrist bones to secure Him to the cross. We often think of the scars as being on His hands, but in reality the nails went through His wrists. The scars on His wrists and feet represent His crushed body. As believers, you and I are marked with the Holy Spirit. There may not be an outward mark visible to others that we are in covenant with Christ, but Jesus said people could identify believers by the fruit of their lives: joy, peace, patience, goodness, kindness, and self-control.

The seventh step in the covenant-making process was the pronouncement of blessings and curses. This occurred in the presence of witnesses. The parties faced each other and said, "So long as you keep the terms of this covenant, blessed shall you be when you go out and when you come in. Blessed shall you be when you rise up and when you lay down. Blessed shall be your wife, blessed shall be your children, blessed shall be all that you put your hands to."
The culture in biblical times revolved around agriculture. The parties would finish by saying, "Blessed shall be your oxen,

your donkeys, your fields, and the produce of your fields." There would be a pause. The ceremony would end with both parties saying, "But if you violate the terms of this covenant, cursed shall you be when you rise up and lay down. Cursed shall be your wife, your children. Cursed shall be your oxen, your donkeys, and your land."

In a traditional Christian marriage each couple usually professes their commitment to one another by announcing their vows in front of the congregation. Even through marriage can be hard; the Bible considers it a blessing. Scripture says it is not good for man to be alone, and if he finds a wife, he has found a good thing. The blessing of marriage is the oneness that comes from entering into a covenant with God and your partner. Scripture views marriage as a holy covenant before God.

In a traditional Jewish wedding, the couple signs an agreement to seal the marriage covenant. This agreement, or marriage contract, is called a *ketubah*. By signing this agreement, the husband accepts responsibilities such as providing food, shelter, and clothing for his family and agrees to meet his wife's emotional needs. The marriage ceremony is a public demonstration of a couple's commitment to a covenant relationship. The contract says the relationship is not only physically and legally binding, but emotionally and spiritually binding as well. As for a traditional Christian marriage ceremony, cutting covenant is a divine picture of the relationship between Christ and His church, or bride. It is a spiritual representation of our relationship with the Lord.

The eighth step in the process was the covenant meal. The covenant partners sat at a table before their witnesses and shared a meal. However, the parties didn't begin the meal by feeding themselves; they first fed each other. How many husbands and wives have pictures of the moment they first fed each other a piece of the wedding cake before serving themselves?

> Jesus said to them, "I tell you the truth, unless you eat the flesh of the Son of Man and drink his blood, you have no life in you. Whoever eats my flesh and drinks my blood has eternal life, and I will raise him up at the last day. For my flesh is real food and my blood is real drink. Whoever eats my flesh and drinks my blood remains in me, and I in him. Just as the living Father sent me and I live because of the Father, so the one who feeds on me will live because of me.
> —John 6:53–57 NIV

Of course the most famous covenant meal is the Last Supper: "In the same way, after supper He took the cup, saying, 'This cup is the new covenant in my blood; do this, whenever you drink it, in remembrance of me'" (1 Cor. 11:25 NIV).

The ninth covenant step was a name exchange. The partners again stood facing each other and exchanged names. The name change is precisely what occurred when God made a covenant with Abram. God changed Abram's name to Abraham. And then we see God taking on Abraham's name. From this point, He called Himself "the God of Abraham." I get chills thinking that the God of the universe would call Himself the God of a man. "No longer will you be called Abram; your name will be Abraham, for I have made you a father of many nations" (Gen. 17:5 NIV).

As a wife, I took my husband's last name, symbolizing the oneness and melting of identities in the marriage covenant.

As believers, once we enter into a covenant relationship with God through Jesus Christ, we are washed in His blood. All past, present, and future sins are forgiven. God's identity becomes our identity, God's strength becomes our strength, and God's weapons become our weapons. The choice between blessings and curses becomes ours, and we inherit new names as children of God. This name can be called *Christian*.

As a child of God, your new name is Christian! The word is found only three times in the New Testament (Acts 11:26; Acts 26:28; 1 Peter 4:16) as the name given to the disciples or followers of Christ at Antioch. Some think *Christian* means *little Christ*. In fact, the word means bearing the name of Christ our Lord. You take on a new name and a new identity. The name carries the idea of a Christ or one belonging to Christ. This new name gives us a whole new responsibility for how we conduct ourselves based upon whom we represent.

The tenth and final step of the covenant was the exchange of the oldest male child in the family. According to tradition, to prove that the covenant was for real, the partners would exchange their oldest sons. Can you imagine? A son would move into the home of the covenant partner and be raised by that family. This must have been extremely painful, but proved that the covenant was genuine. We see Abraham living out the last step of the covenant when God asked him to sacrifice his only son. A promised son he had awaited for so long—now the Lord was asking Abraham to sacrifice this son as a burnt offering.

> Some time later God tested Abraham. He said
> to him, "Abraham!" "Here I am," he replied.
> Then God said, "Take your son, your only son,
> whom you love—Isaac—and go to the region
> of Moriah. Sacrifice him there as a burnt offering
> on a mountain I will show you."
>
> —Gen. 22:1–2 NIV

Hebrews 11:17–19 tells us that in his heart Abraham had already sacrificed Isaac, knowing that God was able to raise him up from the dead. How did Abraham justify doing this in his mind? How painful it must have been to know that he was about to sacrifice his only son. Someone he loved so much and would do anything for, even to the point of death, was now being taken away from him. But Abraham's faith in the Lord was so strong that he held on to the covenant promise that his heir would bring the Messiah. And if God was asking him to sacrifice Isaac, then God was capable of raising Isaac from the dead.

Abraham had such strong faith in God's Word that he was willing to give up his son. He could raise his hand and put a knife through Isaac's heart, knowing that God would raise the boy from the dead—because God had made a covenant promise that through this seed He would bless the nations.

Genesis 22:4 NIV notes that "on the third day Abraham lifted up his eyes, and saw the place afar off." When we read this verse, we see that Abraham had already emotionally detached himself from Isaac. Figuratively speaking, Isaac had already been dead for three days in Abraham's mind. God resurrected him, figuratively, on the third day. "By faith Abraham, when God tested him, offered Isaac as a sacrifice.

He who had embraced the promises was about to sacrifice his one and only son" (Heb.11: 17 NIV).

Scripture tells us that God knows His children. He knows the number of hairs on our heads, and He knows what we are going to say before we say it. In other words, God knows our hearts and our thought processes. God knew the way Abraham was thinking. Abraham was going to be obedient to God by sacrificing his son, but still he held on to the promise that the Messiah would come through Abraham's descendants. Abraham's confidence in God's covenant was so great that he believed God would resurrect Isaac from the dead.

God stopped Abraham at the last second. This test revealed Abraham's heart to God. It revealed his confidence, his trust, and his commitment to God. Because of Abraham's faith, God declared him righteous. Isaac, who lay dead in Abraham's heart for three days, connects us to Jesus' body being in the tomb for three days before His resurrection. Everything in the Bible points us to Jesus' story, His death, and His resurrection.

Scripture tells us that husbands are to love their wives as Christ loves the church, which is sacrificially, to the point of death. It is interesting that wives are not called to love their husbands, but to respect them, and husbands are called to a love so deep that they would be willing to die for their wives. That is amazing. A man capable of such love deserves respect!

I pray that the Holy Spirit opens our eyes to see this, understand it, and give us daily wisdom to live a holy life.

In *The Spirit-Filled Family*, Jack W. Hayford writes,

The covenant of marriage is the single most important human bond that holds all of God's work on the planet together. It is no small wonder that the Lord is passionate about the sanctity of marriage and the stability of the home. This covenant of marriage is based on the covenant God has made with us. It is in the power of His promise to mankind that our personal covenant of marriage can be kept against the forces that would destroy homes and ruin lives.[11]

---

11   Jack Hayford, "The Covenant of Marriage," The Spirit-Filled Family, P-R-E-C-E-P-T A-U-S-T-I-N http://www.preceptaustin.org/the_covenant_of_marriage.htm (accessed June 28, 2012).

chapter 2

OUR COVENANT WITH JESUS

For whoever wants to save their life will lose it; but whoever loses their life for me will find it. What good will it be for someone to gain the whole world, yet forfeit their soul? Or what can anyone give in exchange for their soul?

—Matt. 16:25–26 NIV

Why would Jesus say we could not live unless we die first? What did He mean when He said we must lose our lives for His sake? As our covenant partner, He is calling us to walk the walk of death, death to our independent living and ourselves. As Christians, our eternity is sealed, but what is our role as Jesus' covenant partners here on earth? Has society developed a theology that says we can be Christians but not be committed to Christ? In a covenant relationship, neither partner belongs to himself any longer. Two become one. What stands out most in this part of the covenant process is the walk of death. We could view this as a daily walk in which we choose to put God first, not ourselves.

> But seek first his kingdom and his righteousness,
> and all these things will be given to you as well.
> —Matt. 6:33 NIV

In *My Utmost for His Highest*, Oswald Chambers writes the following about this verse:

> Immediately we look at these words of Jesus, we find them the most revolutionary statement human ears ever listened to. "Seek ye *first* the kingdom of God." We argue in exactly the opposite way, even the most spiritually minded of us—"But I *must* live; I *must* make so much money; I *must* be clothed; I *must* be fed." The great concern of our lives is not the kingdom of God, but how we are to fit ourselves to live. Jesus reverses the order: Get rightly related to God first, maintain that as the great care of your life, and never put the concern of your care on the other things.
> *"Take no thought for your life ... "* Our Lord points out the utter unreasonableness from His standpoint of being so anxious over the means of living. Jesus is not saying that the man who takes thought for nothing is blessed—that man is a fool. Jesus taught that a disciple has to make his relationship to God the dominating concentration of his life, and to be carefully careless about everything else in comparison to that. Jesus is saying, "Don't make the ruling factor of your life what you shall eat and what you shall drink, but be concentrated absolutely on God." Some people are careless over what

they eat and drink, and they suffer for it; they are careless about what they wear, and they look as they have no business to look; they are careless about their earthly affairs, and God holds them responsible. Jesus is saying that the great care of the life is to put the relationship to God first, and everything else second.

It is one of the severest disciplines of the Christian life to allow the Holy Spirit to bring us into harmony with the teaching of Jesus in these verses.[12]

Chambers calls putting God first a spiritual discipline. It is not something that comes naturally; it is a choice. Our covenant partner can point out the way that we should go, but it is up to us to follow. God chose to give His one and only Son as a sacrifice to atone for all sin. Jesus went on His own accord to the cross in complete submission to His Father's plan.

In the Old Testament, Isaac, unaware that he was the intended victim, probably carried the wood up Mount Moriah to sacrifice his own body. Likewise, Jesus carried the wood of the cross, intended for the sacrifice of His own body, up the hill of Calvary to a place known as Golgotha, or Place of the Skull. Jesus tells His followers to pick up their crosses and follow Him. What is your cross? What is your sacrifice? What is the burden that requires all your strength to tell the Lord, "Not my will but your will be done"?

12　　Oswald Chambers, "Drawing on the Grace of God-Now," RBC Ministries, http://www.utmost.org/classic/divine-reasonings-of-faith-classics/ (accessed June 29, 2012).

According to covenant custom in Abraham's day, the partners walked through the bloody pieces of sacrificed animals, then called upon God to take the life of the man who broke the covenant. This "walk of death" represented one's commitment to the other.

A committed follower of Jesus Christ is called a disciple. Can one be a Christian and not be a disciple of Jesus Christ? Can one be committed to Christ but not follow Him? The word *disciple* is very much a part of the Christian faith. The word is used 262 times in the New Testament. The Greek root word is *mathetes,* meaning *learner* or *pupil.* The term *disciple* is basically absent from the Old Testament, but in the New Testament it describes one who shares a close and intimate relationship with a person.

A disciple of any trade or school of thought understands that there is commitment and dedication involved to study and pursue their mentor's teachings. Therefore a Christian disciple is one who is more than a believer in Jesus Christ. As a disciple of Jesus Christ one should be committed to studying His word. We know God speaks through His word. God's word will reveal the truth to be applied to our everyday lives. God's word will strengthen our faith and guide our hearts in the right direction. A true disciple of Jesus knows that His word is alive and active, sharper than a double-edge sword. When one chooses to study the Word they are studying Jesus himself.

In *The Cost of Discipleship,* John MacArthur writes,

> Discipleship ... more than just being a learner, being an intimate follower, having an intimate relationship, following to the point where you would go as far as death out of love. There's no

question about the fact that the only message Jesus ever proclaimed was a message of discipleship. The call that Jesus gave was a call to follow Him, a call to submission, and a call to obedience. It was never a plea to make some kind of momentary decision to acquire forgiveness and peace and Heaven and then go on living any way you wanted. The invitations of Jesus to the lost were always direct calls to a costly commitment.[13]

So can a Christian think of himself as something other than a disciple? Can the words *Christian* and *disciple* be separated?

In my opinion, if we are Christians, we are followers of Jesus Christ. What did Jesus say to those who called themselves His followers? When Jesus called His disciples, He also called the nearby crowds. He addressed everyone with the call to follow Him. Jesus' words were not just to His disciples, but also to all who considered themselves His followers. His words were directed to those who were considering following Him, curious about who He was, or interested in knowing more about Him and God. Jesus addressed the multitudes to let them know that if they chose to follow Him, this is what they needed to consider. And if you are already a follower of Jesus Christ, the cross is a part of your journey. When we make a conscience choice to become a Christian we then become a disciple and a disciple of Jesus will always have a cross to bear.

Then he called the crowd to him along with his disciples and said: "Whoever wants to be my

13   John MacArthur, "The Cost of Discipleship," Grace to You, http://www.gty.org/resources/sermons/90-23 (accessed June 7, 2012).

disciple must deny themselves and take up their cross and follow me."

—Mark 8:34 NIV

John Wesley's *Explanatory Notes* say this:

> "And when He called the people"—To hear a truth of the last importance, and one that equally concerned them all.
>
> "Let him deny himself"—His own will, in all things small and great, however pleasing, and that continually:
>
> "And take up his cross"—Embrace the will of God, however painful, daily, hourly, continually. "Thus only can he follow Me in holiness to glory."[14]

It takes faith to put aside selfish ambitions and deny fleshly desires in order to follow Christ. To overcome ourselves, we must return to the object of our faith: Jesus Christ.

Faith means believing in something or someone, but a Christian must ask, "What is the object of my faith?" As believers in Jesus Christ, as followers or disciples, our faith is in God through Christ. Hebrews 11:1 NIV provides the definition of faith: "Now faith is being sure of what we hope for and certain of what we do not see." Our hope is in Jesus Christ, whom we cannot literally see.

Does it matter how much faith we have? According to Jesus, it is not a matter of how much faith we have as long as our faith is in Him. "I tell you the truth, if you have faith as small as a mustard seed, you can say to this mountain, 'Move from here

---

14   John Wesley, "Mark 8," Bible Study Tools, http://www.biblestudytools .com/ commentaries/wesleys...notes/mark/makr-8.html (accessed June 27, 2012).

to there,' and it will move. Nothing will be impossible for you" (Matt. 17:20 NIV).

Our faith is in the God of the universe, the God who made all things. The God who used his own hands to stretch out the heavens and lays the foundation of the earth. The stars reside at his command. He gives breath to his people and life to those who choose to walk in it. Jesus said that if your faith resides in Him then nothing would be impossible for you.

To follow Jesus and put our faith in him will cause us to put aside, overlook or even reject the plans or agenda we have for ourselves.

The more time we spend in the Word, in prayer, and around other believers, the more our desires begin to change. God will use everything in our lives to conform us more and more into the image of His Son. Will we join Him? Being a disciple of Christ means we must trust that His plan for our lives is better than the one we have for ourselves. Will we trust Him?

There is a familiar story about a tightrope walker in Paris who did incredible stunts. He would perform tightrope acts at tremendously scary heights. He would walk the tightrope blindfolded, and the crowd would go wild. Then he would walk across the tightrope blindfolded pushing a wheelbarrow, and the crowd would really go wild.

An American promoter read about this man in the newspapers and wrote a letter, saying, "Mr. Tightrope Walker, I do not believe you can do this, but I'm willing to make you an offer. For a very substantial amount of money, besides your transportation fees, I would like to challenge you to do your act over Niagara Falls."

Mr. Tightrope Walker wrote back and said, "Sir, I'd love to come."

After much promotion and logistical work, the event was set and a crowd of people came to see it. Mr. Tightrope Walker started on the Canadian side and walked to the American side on a rope suspended over the rolling white water. With a suspenseful drum roll, he came across blindfolded. The crowd went wild! He said to the promoter, "Well, Mr. Promoter, now do you believe I can do it?"

The promoter said, "Well, of course I do. I just saw you do it."

"No," said Mr. Tightrope Walker. "Do you really believe I can do it?"

"Of course I do; you just did it!"

"No, no, no!" said Mr. Tightrope Walker. "Do you believe I can do it?"

"Yes," Mr. Promoter conceded, "I believe you can do it."

"Good," said Mr. Tightrope Walker. "Then get in the wheelbarrow."

Our faith is not just something to be discussed. It must be demonstrated by the way we live. Someone once said, "If you don't live it, you don't believe it." There's biblical basis for that statement. James said, "Show me your faith without your works, and I will show you my faith by my works" (James 2:18 ESV).

Are you willing to get in the wheelbarrow? That takes a lot of faith, but if Jesus Christ is the one pushing the wheelbarrow, we must take comfort that our lives are in suitable hands. Your covenant partner, Jesus, will uphold you with His righteous right hand. If life were a tightrope walk, I would want no one else pushing me ahead into the unknown.

Getting into the wheelbarrow is the first step to denying ourselves. And if we are in covenant with Jesus Christ, we are in covenant with God. Jesus said, "If you have seen Me, you have seen the Father." Sit back and enjoy the ride.

> When you come to the edge of all the light you know, and are about to step off into the darkness of the unknown, faith is knowing one of two things will happen: There will be something solid to stand on, or you will be taught how to fly.[15]
>
> —Barbara J. Winter

New Self vs. Old Self

You may say, "I'm in the wheelbarrow; I've given my life to Christ and He is in control." I have, too, but our spiritual progress, development, and discipleship are an ongoing process. Being a disciple means we are constantly learning, constantly following, constantly changing to become more like Christ. I hope and pray that who I am today spiritually will not be who I am five or ten years from now. I hope I can look back every year and realize that I know God better. Part of

---

15   Barbara J. Winter, "Quotes," STANDS4LCL, (accessed June 25, 2012).

Jesus' role as our covenant partner is to bring us through this process.

> As we know Jesus better, his divine power gives
> us everything we need for living a godly life.
> --2 Peter 1:3 NLT

My husband and I enjoy playing golf together. One of my challenges is alignment. If you are a golfer, you know that golf is a target game. Before every stroke, you must align your body to hit the target. Feet, knees, hips, and shoulders must be lined up appropriately to accomplish this goal.

There are times when my shoulders are pointed one way and my hips the other. At impact, the clubface is open and I miss my target. My sweet husband patiently reminds me that I don't have to focus so much on my target as I do on aligning to the target before I hit the ball. If I don't align myself to hit the target, it won't happen. My focus should be on the alignment process, not so much where I want to hit the ball. If I'm properly aligned, I will have confidence to swing away, knowing I've done my part.

Only Jesus knows the target, only Jesus knows the goal, and only Jesus knows the life He has planned for us. But we must do our part to align ourselves with everything God has given us to seek out His plan for our lives. For our minds to be renewed and for transformation to occur, we must do our best to do our part. We have control of reading God's Word daily, memorizing Scripture, meditating, and praying without ceasing. By pursuing such things we are aligning ourselves to the target! We may be pulling out the diver on a par five and the flag is nowhere in sight. But we don't have to worry about slicing or hooking the ball. We've aligned ourselves the best we know how to follow Christ. Scripture teaches that you and I are works in progress. Jesus says, "But seek first the Kingdom of God and his righteousness, and all these things will be added to you (Matt. 6:33 ESV). If we do our best to put God first, He will take care of the rest. What we choose to put in our minds will always affect our attitude, behavior, and beliefs.

The Bible says that God's Word is alive and active. It has the power to change our way of thinking. To allow the Holy Spirit to control our minds, we must allow Him into our thought process. We must be aware of any negative thoughts that do not line up with Scripture. This takes work and discipline.

> Therefore, I urge you, brothers, in view of God's mercy, to offer your bodies as living sacrifices, holy and pleasing to God—this is your spiritual act of worship. Do not conform any longer to the pattern of this world, but be transformed by the renewing of your mind. Then you will be able to test and approve what God's will is—His good, pleasing, and perfect will.
>
> —Rom. 12:1–2 NIV

If we analyze this verse, we can see a call to a walk of death and a renewing of the mind. How can a sacrifice be living? Jesus says we must die to ourselves, but think of it as living for Him. In the Old Testament, God minutely detailed how animal sacrifices were to be presented to Him. God would accept only the best the people could give; no damaged, blemished, hurt, or deformed animals would be acceptable. Jesus Christ met the standard of the spotless lamb, the perfect sacrifice for the atonement of sin. Now God asks you and me to offer our lives to Him in His service. We must crawl up on God's altar and willingly sacrifice our fleshly desires. In return, He will give us His desires.

We are no longer to conform to the pattern of this world. This is a warning not to surrender to the worldly culture that opposes God's will for our lives. How is it possible to resist the world? The Holy Spirit makes it possible for believers to keep their thoughts whole, pure, positive, and constructive. Daily we must empty our minds of toxic thoughts and replace them with the things of God. The word *renew* could be translated as *renovating*. According to *Vine's Expository Dictionary of New Testament Words*, the "renewing of the Holy Spirit" mentioned in Titus 3:5 "is not a fresh bestowment of the Spirit, but a revival of His power."[16]

The Greek word for *transformed* is *metamorphosis*, the scientific name for the change of a clumsy caterpillar into a delicate butterfly. In school, we studied how a caterpillar becomes a butterfly. The transformation brings a complete change. When a hungry larvae hatches from its egg, it begins to move forward, munching on whatever it can find. It will eat leaves on trees or on the ground. At maturity, it spins a cocoon.

What happens in the cocoon is amazing! The awkward, lumbering caterpillar emerges as a beautiful butterfly. It is totally changed in its very nature. It is a new creature! No longer is it bound to the ground, eating leaves. No longer is it in a state of sleep, locked in a cocoon. After its metamorphosis, it is free to fly from flower to flower, eating sweet nectar. As

---

16   Vine's Expository Dictionary of New Testament Words, "Renew, Renewing (Verb and Noun)- Vine's Expository Dictionary of New Words, bible@ studybible.info, http://www.studybible.info/vine/Renew,%20Renewing%20 (verb%20and%20noun),(accessed June 28, 2012).

a new creature, the butterfly offers delight to all as it flashes its beautiful colors, enjoying the freedom to fly where it pleases.

In Christ, the believer is a new creation, but transformation is an ongoing process. The believer receives a new mind, the mind of Christ, but is not transformed overnight. Leaving the cocoon, the caterpillar sheds its skin; this is called molting. Partial change will not work for the caterpillar; complete change must occur. Because the Holy Spirit dwells within the Christian, sanctification is continual. The Spirit desires the things of God for you and me.

If the caterpillar lived his whole life in the cocoon, the molting process would never occur and a beautiful butterfly would not come into being. Living in a cocoon is not enough for us. God knows what we are to become and how we are meant to be—like the beautiful, free butterfly. We are works in progress as we learn how to forgive, how to treat others, and how to put our hope in Christ and experience freedom in doing so. You could look at the cocoon as the old self and the butterfly as the new self. The cocoon must be shed.

If we must die to ourselves, what exactly is God asking us to die to? What must we become to live for Him? Read Ephesians and see if you can identify transformation from the old self to the new self. Listen and look for change. See if you can recognize areas where you have put off the old you for the new you. Where is the Holy Spirit nudging you to move?

> Now this I say and testify in the Lord, that you must no longer walk as the Gentiles do, in the futility of their minds. They are darkened in their understanding, alienated from the life of God

because of the ignorance that is in them, due to their hardness of heart. They have become callous and have given themselves up to sensuality, greedy to practice every kind of impurity. But that is not the way you learned Christ! —Assuming that you have heard about Him and were taught in Him, as the truth is in Jesus, to put off your old self, which belongs to your former manner of life and is corrupt through deceitful desires, and to be renewed in the spirit of your minds, and to put on the new self, created after the likeness of God in true righteousness and holiness.

Therefore, having put away falsehood let each one of you speak the truth with his neighbor, for we are members of one another. Be angry and do not sin; do not let the sun go down on your anger, and give no opportunity to the devil. Let the thief no longer steal, but rather let him labor, doing honest work with his own hands, so that he may have something to share with anyone in need. Let no corrupt talk come out of your mouths, but only such as is good for building up, as fits the occasion, that it may give grace to those who hear. And do not grieve the Holy Spirit of God, by whom you were sealed for the day of redemption.

Let all bitterness and wrath and anger and clamor and slander be put away from you, along with all malice. Be kind to one another, tenderhearted, forgiving one another, as God in Christ forgave you. Therefore, be imitators of God, as beloved children. And walk in love, as Christ loved us and gave Himself up for a fragrant offering, a sacrifice and us to God.

—Eph. 4:17–5:2 ESV

The Mind of Christ

If we are in Christ, we have the mind of Christ in us. Jesus, as our covenant partner, resides in us—in our hearts and minds. When we were created in our mother's wombs, we were created with a body, a soul, and a spirit. You could refer to this spirit inside of us as our "inner spirit-man." Our physical body is obvious; our soul consists of our emotions, personality, and passions; our spirit is our inner spirit-man.

When we receive Jesus as our Lord and Savior, His Spirit, the Holy Spirit, enters into us and connects with our inner spirit-man. Christ comes to dwell in us and becomes one with our spirit. The spirit in us is united with the Holy Spirit of God. "But the person who is joined to the Lord becomes one spirit with Him" (1 Cor. 6:17 NLT).

Because of our covenant relationship, Jesus is committed to our spiritual maturity. He is committed to changing our way of thinking to His way of thinking. The apostle Paul urged all believers to strive for maturity in their way of thinking: "Brothers and sisters, stop thinking like children. In regard to evil be infants, but in your thinking be adults" (1 Cor. 14:20 NIV). This process cannot occur by our own doing; it is the work of God in our lives, exchanging our desire for this world for a desire for holiness.

The Psalmist said, "Taste and see that the Lord is good." Have you tasted to see that the Lord wants good things for you?

The Psalmist, David, also said that he hid Scripture in his heart so that he would not sin against God. One of the many characteristics of the Holy Spirit is that He searches all things. We know that God searches the earth to and fro looking for hearts committed to Him. We know that God looks at the heart of a man, not the outer appearance. He judges hearts and motives. The Spirit of God inside us searches all things, even the deep things of God. And who else would know the thoughts of God other than God? (1 Cor. 2:10–11NIV)

We see here an important characteristic of the Spirit of God: He is a searcher. In other words, if the Holy Spirit resides within us, there will be a longing in us for the things of God. Will we give in to the longing and join?

Consider, for example, a believer caught in a habitual sin, such as an addiction. We are told in 2 Peter that a believer will be more miserable than an unbeliever over a sin that is entangling him. Because the Holy Spirit convicts us of our sin, we realize that remaining in our sin grieves the Lord. Disregarding or disobeying the promptings of our Savior and Lord will make us miserable. We have the Spirit of God inside us striving for holiness and sanctification. When we choose to ignore this call, we are denying God Himself.

That can be a scary thing! When I am away from the things of God, there is an ache, a feeling of emptiness inside me that I cannot shake. Everything in life may be perfect and orderly, but inside I am dissatisfied. I have a longing on the inside to connect with Jesus again.

Likewise, you may have a great husband, a beautiful wife, healthy kids, and a great job, but you are still searching for something that you cannot quite identify. Perhaps the God of the universe is telling you that He wants you to go deeper with Him. Perhaps He wants to enrich your prayer life and use you to help Him reconcile a lost world to Himself. When we get away from the things of God, our covenant partner will always run after us and bring us back.

> Therefore gird up the loins of your mind, be sober, and rest your hope fully upon the grace that is to be brought to you at the revelation of Jesus Christ.
> —I Peter 1:13 NKJV

Edward Mote penned these words:

My hope is built on nothing less
Than Jesus' blood and righteousness;
I dare not trust the sweetest frame,
But wholly trust in Jesus' Name

When darkness veils His lovely face,
I rest on His unchanging grace;
In every high and stormy gale,
My anchor holds within the veil.

His oath, His covenant, His blood,
Support me in the whelming flood;
When all around my soul gives way,
He then is all my Hope and Stay.

When He shall come with trumpet sound,
Oh, may I then in Him be found;
Dressed in His righteousness alone,
Faultless to stand before the throne.

On Christ the solid Rock I stand,
All other ground is sinking sand;
All other ground is sinking sand.[17]

---

17   Edward Mote, "The Solid Rock," Lively Salt, http://www.library.timelesstruth. org/music/The_Solid_Rock/ (accessed June 29, 2012).

chapter 3

COVENANT ADOPTION

You are all children of God through faith in Christ Jesus, for all of you who were baptized into Christ have clothed yourselves with Christ. There is neither Jew nor Greek, slave nor free, male nor female, for you are all one in Christ Jesus. If you belong to Christ, then you are Abraham's seed, and heirs according to the promise.

—Gal. 3:26–29 NIV

I played in a charity golf tournament for the Homes of St. Mark, an adoption agency of fifty-two years. On each tee box were pictures of children who had been adopted; their stories were written for all to read.

I believe God has a special place in His heart for orphans. Isaiah 1:17 NLT tells us, "Learn to do good. Seek justice. Help the oppressed. Defend the orphan. Fight for the rights of widows." Here we see what is good in the eyes of God.

I spoke to the social workers at Homes of St. Mark, and each one told me of the potential neglect, physical, emotional, and verbal abuse that older orphaned children could have endured prior to adoption. She said there were a lot of older children who longed to be with a forever home. How this broke my heart! So many children need someone to love them unconditionally. Would they ever experience the love and security that comes from knowing no matter what they do or where they have been, they are loved, special, and unique?

I'm sure that every adoptive parent cannot wait to bond with his or her child. Every parent longs to connect and to grow a strong relationship by showing love, trust, and genuine affection. Scripture tells us we all were created to live in community with others and with God. We were made to connect to other people. All adoptive parents want their children to adapt to new surroundings. They do not want the children to become anxious or fearful, but they want them to learn to trust that they are in a safe place. I am not an expert on this by any means, but my heart breaks to see so many innocent children in need of families who will give them this opportunity. When a family adopts a child, what joy must come to the family's heart—and to God's heart, knowing that one of His children has been given a loving, caring home.

No parent is perfect. We can look back at the mistakes our parents made and the ones we have made ourselves. We know, however, that love covers a multitude of sins. At our salvation, or at the moment we accept Jesus Christ as our savior, several things happen in the spiritual realm. Spiritually speaking, when one becomes a Christian and believes in Jesus Christ, one is adopted into a whole new family, the family of God.

All of us are born with a sinful nature. No one has to teach us how to sin or operate out of the flesh. Romans 3:23 tell us that all of us have sinned and fallen short of the glory of God. And because of our sinful nature, we are separated from the

Father. But by sending His Son to take our place, to die on the cross, and pay the penalty for our sin, the Father has given us a way to Him. Jesus says, "I am the way, the truth and the life; no one can go to the Father except through Me (John 14:6 NIV). Because of the Father's great love, Jesus took on the sin of the world, past, present, and future.

Scripture tells us we are justified through faith. Justification is the divine exchange whereby Jesus' blood covers us and makes it as though we never sinned in God's eyes. We are in essence born again, and God takes our old, dirty rags and replaces them with new, clean, beautiful robes. Our sin that was once as red as crimson is now as white as snow with our new birth, our new life, our new hope. And we are then members of a new family. We are adopted into the kingdom of God. "And because we are His children, God has sent forth the Spirit of His Son into our hearts, prompting us to call out 'Abba, Father!'" (Gal. 4:6 NLT)

The word *father* can evoke different feelings in different people. Some may associate an earthly father with feelings of fear, rejection, instability, disappointment, or abandonment. Others may have had fathers who were kind, loving, and gentle and pursued relationships with them. Since we all had imperfect parents, we must not allow unhappy experiences to form our understanding of the heavenly Father. I wonder if daddies realize that they are the first image of God that their children have!

When we are adopted into the family of God, we receive the ultimate Father. Scriptures say God is willing to give anything to save us: "He who did not spare His own Son, but gave Him up for us all—how will He not also, along with Him, graciously give us all things?" (Rom. 8:32 NIV) He is ready and willing to meet all our needs. "Which of you fathers, if your son asks for a fish, will give him a snake instead? Or if he asks for an egg, will give him a scorpion? If you then, though you are evil, know how to give good gifts to your children, how much more will your Father in heaven give the Holy Spirit to those who ask him!" (Luke 11:11–13 NIV)

Your Heavenly Father also cares enough to discipline you. "And you have forgotten that word of encouragement that addresses you as sons: 'My son, do not make light of the Lord's discipline, and do not lose heart when He rebukes you, because the Lord disciplines those He loves and He punishes everyone He accepts as a son'" (Heb. 12:6–10 NIV). Paul goes on to say that if our Heavenly Father does not discipline us, then we are not legitimate children of God.

Randy Pausch, a computer science professor at Carnegie Mellon University, delivered a lecture titled "Really Achieving Your Childhood Dreams." He was dying of pancreatic cancer and wrote this lecture for his three children. It became the basis for his book *The Last Lecture*.

In the lecture, Pausch recalled playing multiple sports growing up. He always seemed to be getting in trouble with his coaches and having to pay the consequences. He remembered running laps until he was out of breath, falling down, and almost vomiting.   Pausch said it didn't matter to him how his coaches disciplined him as much as the fact that they did. He said if the day had come when his coaches gave up on him and didn't care about his screw-ups or mistakes, this would have been a day to mourn. The day when someone stops caring about you is the day he will not make the effort to put you back on the right path.

Hearing Pausch, I immediately thought of God as a heavenly Father whose motive in disciplining His children is to grow them to spiritual maturity. He will never give up on any of His children, no matter how many mistakes and wrong moves they make. He will either gently redirect or boldly push them back to where they should be. When we rebel, reject, or ignore His ways, we will reap what we sow, but God will continue to love us unconditionally.

We know that He loves us even when we don't love Him. "We love because he first loved us" (I John 4:19 NIV). As Christians, we too can feel distant or unworthy of love from God based on our relationship with our earthly fathers. If we did not experience unconditional love with an earthly father, we must discover who our heavenly Father is and what He wants for His children.

We have been adopted as sons and daughters, and our heavenly Father says we can call Him daddy. You say, "Call Him daddy? That sounds so childlike." Galatians 4:6 says because you are a son or a daughter of God, the Holy Spirit resides in your heart and there will be heard a cry of "Abba, Father." Another word for *abba* is *daddy*. It is an intimate word for *father*. A daddy cares deeply for his child. A daddy gives all of himself to meet his child's needs. A daddy protects and listens and carries us when we can't carry ourselves. A daddy will let us know he loves us when we don't feel lovable. A daddy puts forth effort to discipline his children because he knows it will create a since of security in their lives. A daddy would lay down his life for his children.

Because of our spiritual adoption, we can cry out "Abba, Father!" and know there is a daddy God who will extend His mercy and grace to meet whatever need we have.

Not only will He meet the need for unconditional love, but the need for companionship and security. "Never will I leave you; never will I forsake you" (Heb. 13:5 NIV). How many people can say this and mean it? Because of covenant, this relationship is a permanent one. Jesus promises that no one can ever snatch us out of His hand (John 10:28 NIV). Therefore we can rest in the knowledge that we are children of God forever.

As children of God, not only do we receive a new Father, but we also receive a new inheritance. "So you are no longer a slave, but God's child; and since you are His child, God has made you also an heir" (Gal. 4:7 NIV). We will never really know all that becomes ours until we get to heaven. It is impossible for us to understand what heaven is really like while we are still here on earth. How can we comprehend what it means to be a fellow heir with Jesus?

I read this Scripture and cannot grasp the reality that I could be even remotely deserving of anything equal to our Lord. But Jesus said His inheritance is ours. He said we didn't deserve it, but He died for it. He died so that we can join Him in heaven. It is hard to understand, but the Holy Spirit will convince us that we are indeed children of the Most High King. "The Spirit himself testifies with our spirit that we are God's children. Now if we are children, then we are heirs—heirs of God and co-heirs with Christ, if indeed we share in his sufferings in order that we may also share in his glory" (Rom. 8:16–17 NIV). The Spirit bears witness that we belong to Jesus. Let the Holy Spirit convince you of the reality that you are a child of the Most High and a fellow heir with Jesus Christ.

As adopted children, we not only receive a new Father, a new family, and a new inheritance, but also new rights. Galatians 4:5 says we "receive the full rights of sons." Being adopted allows us the right to cry out to our heavenly Father at any time. We have the freedom to approach the throne room of God where Jesus sits at the right hand of the Father. The Bible says to pray without ceasing, meaning we are to be in constant communication with Him. God wants to answer the prayers of those whose hearts are completely His (2 Chron. 16:9 NIV). We can go to God confidently with our questions, concerns, needs, and doubts, and He will respond to us in love (Luke 11:5–13 NIV).

As sons and daughters of Christ, we are given the grace to be forgiven. We now have the freedom to be cleansed and made whole. Once we believe in our hearts that the shed blood of the Lamb has forgiven us of our sin, it is also our pleasure and privilege to extend this forgiveness to others.

As children of God, we have the right to rejoice. There is a difference between happiness and joy. Happiness comes from us, but joy comes from the Lord. Our happiness can depend on our circumstances, but no one can steal our joy. Our joy as Christians should not depend on our circumstances. If joy comes from God, it cannot be affected by what others say, do, or don't do. We cannot be fooled into allowing the actions of others to determine our joy. Whatever our circumstances, we know that nothing happens to us that God did not allow, and God will not give us more than we can handle. "Consider it pure joy, my brothers, whenever you face trials of many kinds, because you know that the testing of your faith develops perseverance. Perseverance must finish its work so that you may be mature and complete, not lacking anything" (James 1:2–4 NIV).

Scripture says that the joy of the Lord is also our strength. Have you ever noticed how some people have endured pure hardship yet still maintain their joy? At one time I had a close friend whom I considered my mentor. She had experienced much tragedy in her life. Her first child drowned and then her husband of a young age lost his life. She eventually met someone else and started a family again. She called her husband her prince charming. In knowing her you would have never known her struggles from her past. She was filled with joy, had a spirit of gratitude, and reaching out to younger women to guide them spiritually. I've been around people who have never even come close to experiencing her life's challenges and yet struggle to keep their heads above water. I saw within my Mentor a deep well within her heart that she daily drew fresh, clean, clear, sparkling water from that refreshed herself and those around her. I noticed that this well could not be drained by her circumstances.

It's hard not to allow trying circumstances to cancel out our joy. By choosing to allow God's Spirit to fill us with His seeds of joy we could potentially help someone else who may be experiencing circumstances similar to our own. "The desert shall rejoice and blossom as the rose" (Isa. 35:1 ASV). As we look around us, our circumstances may seem bare, empty, and hopeless like a desert. But God can bring out of our desert something as tender as a rose that can bloom new, fresh, and alive once again.

chapter 4

COVENANT PROTECTION

> The safest place in all the world is in the will of God, and the safest protection in all the world is the name of God. When you know His name, you know His nature. His names and titles reveal His nature. They tell us what He can do and us who He is. For example, He is Jehovah, the God who makes covenants. He is the Lord, the sovereign king. He is Jesus, the Savior. Each name He bears is a blessing He bestows on us.[18]
>
> —Warren Wiersbe

As we have seen, when one moves into covenant with another, one assumes the obligation to come to the partner's defense. The two are now one. They must protect one another from danger. Let us look at the covenant David and Jonathan cut, perhaps the best-known covenant in the Bible. This covenant was made between King Saul's son, Jonathan, and David, anointed by the prophet Samuel to be the next king of Israel.

---

18   Warren Wiersbe, "Safest Protection in the World," oChristian.com, http://www.articles.ochristian.com/article10227.shtml (accessed June 27, 2012).

And Saul said to him, "Whose son are you, young man?" And David answered, "I am the son of your servant Jesse the Bethlehemite." After David had finished talking with Saul, Jonathan became one in spirit with David, and he loved him as himself. From that day Saul kept David with him and did not let him return home to his family. And Jonathan made a covenant with David because he loved him as himself. Jonathan took off the robe he was wearing and gave it to David, along with his tunic and even his sword, his bow and his belt.

—I Sam. 17:58–18:1–4

The Living Bible paraphrase reads, "Jonathan swore to be his blood brother."

In *Blood Covenant,* Henry Clay Trumbull comments:
"From that hour the hearts of David and Jonathan were as one. Jonathan could turn away from father and mother, and could repress all personal ambition, and all purely selfish longings, in proof of his loving fidelity to him who was dear to him as his own blood. His love for David was "wonderful, passing the love of women."[19]

Exchanging armor was a symbolic way of saying that one was now taking on a covenant partner's enemies. His enemies were now your enemies. Whenever one partner was under

---

19   Henry Clay Trumbull, "Blood Covenant" P-R-E-C-E-P-T A-U-S-T-I-N, http://www.preceptaustin.org/covenant_the_exchange_of_robes.htm (accessed June 28, 2012).

attack, it was the other partner's duty to come to his aid to protect him.

When Jonathan and David entered into covenant, Saul was king of Israel. He had been made king because the people of Israel had become dissatisfied with God as their king. They cried out that the nation wanted a physical king, a king who could be seen, touched, and followed. They wanted a king to lead them into battle. The people's motive was selfish: they wanted a king so that Israel could be like other nations.

How it must have broken God's heart to hear the cries of his people for something that was not part of His plan. God's plan was for Israel to be set apart, a holy nation unique among all others. What made Israel unique was that God was its king. It was God who reached down and delivered the Jews out of Egypt. It was God who parted the Red Sea and delivered them from their enemies. It was God who sent manna from heaven and fed the people. Yet they wanted more, so God gave them Saul. Samuel warned the people about having a king.

> So Samuel passed on the Lord's warning to the people. "This is how a king will treat you," Samuel said. "The king will draft your sons into his army and make them run before his chariots. Some will be commanders of his troops, while others will be slave laborers. Some will be forced to plow in his fields and harvest his crops, while others will make his weapons and chariot equipment. The king will take your daughters from you and force them to cook and bake and make perfumes for him. He will take away the best of your fields and vineyards and olive groves and give them to his

own servants. He will want your male and female slaves and demand the finest of your cattle and donkeys for his own use. He will demand a tenth of your flocks, and you will be his slaves. When that day comes, you will beg for relief from this king you are demanding, but the Lord will not help you."

—1 Sam. 8:10–18 NLT

The people did not heed Samuel's warning, and the Lord gave them what they wanted. How many times have we wanted more? How many times, like the people of Israel, do we look at our lives and point out where we think God is not enough, when in reality He gives us just what we need? God gives just enough that we must rely on Him financially, emotionally, even physically. The Lord gives and the Lord takes away just enough to keep proper balance in our lives so we will learn to depend on Him.

Saul started out as a good king. Yet, because Saul willfully disobeyed Him, God chose another king. God chose David, described as a man who sought the heart of God.

When Saul realized that the Spirit of the Lord had left him and was now with David, jealousy overtook him. He made several attempts to kill David, realizing that if David became king, Jonathan never would. Saul was afraid of David; David became Saul's number-one enemy. Saul put David on the front lines of battle, hoping he would not come home. Yet the Spirit of the Lord was with David, and everything he did had great success. Songs were sung about David's victorious battles: "Saul has slain his thousands, and David his ten thousands." This made Saul very angry; his jealousy burned for David. God sent a spirit to torment

Saul. Ironically, the only comfort he received came when David played his harp. In those brief moments, Saul would be at peace. Yet, even as David played his beautiful music, Saul could not control his jealousy. It turned him into a madman. Twice while David played his harp, Saul attacked him with a spear. David had to flee for his life. The jealousy escalated until Saul commanded his servants and Jonathan to assassinate David.

The Bible tells us Jonathan and David had a friendship so deep they cut a covenant, even though Jonathan knew David had been anointed to be the next king. From the start, these two had become close friends, but after cutting covenant, they were like brothers. Twice the Bible says that Jonathan loved David as he loved his own soul.

Jonathan loved David as much as he loved, valued, and respected his own life. I can relate to this because I have a twin sister, and I love her this way. We love our own children in such a way. I can only imagine how Jonathan's heart was torn when his dad, the king, wanted to kill David, his covenant partner. Yet Jonathan honored his covenant with David and refused to follow his father's orders.

Jonathan told David about his father's plan to have him killed. Jonathan was bound in covenant to defend David. Whoever came against David also would have to come against Jonathan, even if it was his own father. Jonathan would stand by David because of their covenant made to defend one another. This covenant included David, Jonathan, and God, and was sealed in blood.

David and Jonathan devised a plan to determine when David would be safe from Saul. He would wait for Jonathan to tell him. David reminded Jonathan of their promise to one another: "As for you, show kindness to your servant, for you have brought him into a covenant with you before the Lord. If I am guilty, then kill me yourself! Why hand me over to your father?" (I Sam. 20:8 NIV)

Jonathan reassured David that he would honor the covenant. "'May the Lord be with you as he used to be with my father. And may you treat me with the faithful love of the Lord as long as I live. But if I die, treat my family with this faithful love, even when the Lord destroys all your enemies.' So Jonathan made a solemn pact with David, saying, 'May the Lord destroy all your enemies from the face of the earth!' And Jonathan made David reaffirm his vow of friendship again, for Jonathan loved David as much as he loved himself" (1 Sam. 20:13–17 NLT).

Jonathan knew he was putting his life at risk by protecting David. Jonathan also knew that the Spirit of the Lord was with David. Jonathan could die protecting David, but he was living up to his covenant vow. Jonathan was reaching out for reassurance. If he died first, would David still honor their covenant? If Jonathan died, would his family members become David's enemies or would he treat them as his own? Jonathan was pleading, "David, if I die in protecting you from my father, please don't allow my children to become your enemies. For God is with you, and I want my children to be on your side."

Seeing each other briefly for the last time, David and Jonathan hugged with tears in their eyes knowing this could be the last time they saw one another. Jonathan told David to go in peace because they had made a covenant in the Lord's name. He reminded David that they had entrusted each other and their children into the Lord's hands forever.

> Enter His gates with thanksgiving and His courts with praise; give thanks to Him and praise His name. For the Lord is good and His love endures forever; his faithfulness continues through all generations.
>
> —Psalm 100:4–5 NIV

God has made a covenant to protect his people. It is easy to think, "Why wasn't I protected from illness? Why didn't He prevent the loss of my child? Why was my home destroyed or my child disabled?" You may be remembering September 11, 2001. Where was God's protection then?

Maybe we won't have these answers this side of heaven, but one day every tear will be wiped away and we will see the perfection of the Lord's kind intention. Through our lives, God is writing a story for others to read. His Word says He will use our pain and suffering for our good and His glory. All things work together for good for those who love God and are called according to His purposes (Rom. 8:28 NIV).

As children of God, we are called to live for His purpose. But at times it is difficult to find His purpose when we face one trial after another. It is hard to look beyond our circumstances to the Lord when we know He has allowed pain in our lives. We may feel like we were put on an island against our will, separated from those we love. Yet, even there, we must stay in touch with God. Jesus says, "If you seek Me with your whole heart, you will find Me." Look up instead of around, and you may see God as you've never seen Him before.

A poem by Bible teacher Jill Briscoe puts it so very well:

Don't waste the pain—
Let it prove thee.
Don't stop the tears—
Let them cleanse thee.
Rest, cease the striving—
Soon you'll be arriving
In His arms.
Don't waste the pain—
Let it drive thee
Deeper into God.
He's waiting,
And you should have
Come sooner.[20]

Seek the Lord while He can be found. Walk in the Spirit; be full of the Spirit; pray in the Spirit; worship in the Spirit. God is spirit. We must worship Him in spirit and in truth. Allow your suffering to drive you deeper into God's presence, and know He is there, waiting. The Psalmist also wrote, "Though You have made me see troubles, many and bitter, You will restore my life again; from the depths of the earth You will again bring me up. You will increase my honor and comfort me once again" (Ps. 71:20–21 NIV).

If you are in the midst of a battle, on an island all by yourself, feeling abandoned or trapped between prison walls, realize you are not alone. Your covenant partner, Jesus, stands with you to fight your battles. How do we allow for this? How do we start? What does this mean, and how can I implement this truth

---

20   Jill Briscoe, *Daily Study Bible for Women* (Wheaton, Illinois 60189: Tyndale House Publishing, 1999) Page 1487.

in my life? These are my questions to the Lord. I don't want to sit on the sidelines in despair as life passes me by. I don't want miss out on the joy that is mine in Christ. What about you? My husband and I had a challenging time becoming pregnant with our twins. Every month I would spiral down in a depth of deep despair. The Lord told me I had to give up the feeling of despair. I was carrying it around with me everywhere I went. I let despair define me. Once I gave it over to the Lord a huge weight was gone. The only way I accomplished this was to praise Him. When the feelings of despair would hit me I would immediately begin to praise Him. He gave me a Bible verse to claim. I memorized the verse and when the feeling of despair would return I would recite it in my head. It was though He was saying to me, "I wil take your pain and despair and in return you need to trust me." That verse was Isaiah 61:3. "To all who mourn in Israel, he will give beauty for ashes, joy instead of mourning, praise instead of despair" (Isa. 61:3 NLT). I was walking around with a hidden pain that no one could see. You could say my heart had a stress fracture.

A *Sports Illustrated* article explains what can happen if a stress fracture is not allowed to heal.

> A stress fracture begins when the shocks and strain of playing a game create microscopic cracks in the outer layers of bone—usually in the legs and feet. If the pounding continues and those crevices, which often go undetected, aren't allowed to heal, they can enlarge. When the cracks become large enough to cause pain, they are stress fractures.[21]

---

21   Richard Demak, "Anatomy of A Stress Fracture," http://www.sportsillustrated. cnn.com/vault/article/magazine/mag1065893/index.htm (accessed June 29, 2012).

The Lord knew the pain in my heat was pounding and enlarging. He wanted to take this pain away. As I praised Him for who He was my strength was restored and I was able to move on. While playing basketball in the eleventh grade I actually experienced a real stress fracture. I was driving toward the basket for a layup and the player blocking me grabbed my jersey, threw me to the ground, and landed on top of me. My left thumb bent all the way back to my wrist and the bone cracked. As I lay on the floor, my hand started shaking, turning red, and swelling. I felt the pounding of blood rushing through a stress fracture. It hurt! I didn't want to cry, but I knew something was seriously wrong.

My opponent said she was sorry and tried to help me up, but I couldn't get up. Perhaps it was the shock of knowing that this was more than a strain or a pulled muscle, both of which I had experienced before. But I had to get up. I had to get off the court so the game could continue. I struggled to stand and walked away, holding my left wrist with my right hand. I couldn't believe I was hurt. I didn't want to be out for the season, unable to play. My joy was instantly gone; depression immediately set in. I didn't choose these circumstances; they chose me.

Most of us can say we didn't choose our circumstances, but here we are. A battle lies ahead; either we are in the midst of it or approaching it. As Christians, we are not immune to a fallen world. Sometimes a circumstance is self-inflicted because of sin in our lives. But we have a defender, a vindicator, and a partner who says that He will never forsake us. Jesus, our covenant partner, tells us not to fear.

Isaiah 41:10 NKJV—"Fear not, for I am with you."
Isaiah 41:13 NKJV—"Fear not, for I will help you."

Isaiah 43:1 KJV—"Fear not: for I have redeemed thee, I have called thee by thy name; thou art mine."
Luke 12:7 KJV—"Fear not therefore: ye are of more value than many sparrows."

The Bible mentions the word *fear* 385 times, and sixty-two times, Scripture says, "Fear not." On twenty-six occasions, the Bible says, "Be not afraid."
Evangelist Kenneth Copeland once said, "Fear tolerated is faith contaminated. Fear will never conquer the enemy."[22]

Jehoshaphat became king of Judah at thirty-five and reigned for twenty-five years. Scripture tells us that he strengthened Judah to stand against any attack from its enemies, of which Israel was the foremost. The first thing Jehoshaphat did was tear down false idols and pagan shrines and destroy the Asherah poles. Next he sent out officials, priests, and Levites to teach the people the Word of God.

One day someone said, "Sir, we have a problem. A vast army of three nations is coming against us from Edom; it is already nearby. Sir, what do we do?" Jehoshaphat was alarmed. He ran to the Lord Himself, and asked that all of Judah observe a fast. The people came to Jerusalem to seek the Lord. When we are in a crisis, we want others to pray for us. Jehoshaphat stood before his people and prayed out loud,

O Lord, God of our ancestors, you alone are the God who is in heaven. You are ruler of all the kingdoms of the earth. You are powerful and

---

22   Kenneth Copeland, "The Healing Word," Nuggets of Wisdom, http://www. savedhealed.com/nuggets.htm (Last Updated 4/4/2012).

mighty; no one can stand against you! O our God, did you not drive out those who lived in this land when your people arrived? And did you not give this land forever to the descendants of your friend Abraham? Your people settled here and built this Temple for you. They said, "Where we are faced with calamity such as war, disease, or famine, we can come to stand in your presence before this Temple where your name is honored. We can cry out to you to save us, and you will hear us and rescue us."

—2 Chron. 20:6–9 NLT

Whatever your battle, seek your covenant partner first for help. Cry out to Him to save you. Seek the Lord while He can be found. Jehoshaphat knew he was powerless against this mighty army. He did not know what to do, but told the Lord he wanted His help. He was depending on God for protection. Jehoshaphat knew that victory over the enemy was beyond his ability, and he asked the Lord to intervene.

After Jehoshaphat called on the Lord for help, he waited for an answer. He called on the nation to fast and pray for him as he sought the Lord's strategy. He took time to hear the voice of God and seek out God's plan of protection for him and his people. The Lord answered his prayers:
"He said, 'Listen, all you people of Judah and Jerusalem! Listen, King Jehoshaphat! This is what the Lord says: Do not be afraid! Don't be discouraged by this mighty army, for the battle is not yours, but God's'" (2 Chron. 20:15 NLT).

The battles we face in life we face with our Lord and Savior, Jesus Christ, our covenant partner. He tells us not to fear, not to tremble or be dismayed, or discouraged. He says to stand firm because he stands with us. When the enemy comes, he not only comes against you and me but also against our covenant God. Many of us go into battle every day fighting with our own strength. We come home at the end of the day tired, worn-out, depressed, strained, and beat up. Knowing that the battle belongs to the Lord, our covenant partner who has vowed to protect us, will provide strength to work through our fears and weaknesses.

On the way into battle, Jehoshaphat stopped his army and said, "Listen to me, all you people of Judah and Jerusalem! Believe in the Lord your God, and you will able to stand firm" (2 Chron. 20:20 NLT).

Jehoshaphat told his people that if they believed they would stand firm in the Lord. Then he appointed singers to walk ahead of the army as it marched into battle. These singers sang praises and extolled God's holy splendor. They sang, "Give thanks to the Lord; His faithful love endures forever!"

At that moment, the armies facing them turned away and began fighting among themselves. Judah was delivered.

It is noteworthy that, even though the Lord fought this battle for His people, they still had to engage in it. They had to get up, get dressed, arm themselves, and march forward in faith, believing that the Lord was going before them. They did not have to lift a finger, but still they had to go to battle.

As they entered the battle, they praised the Lord. The place where they praised the Lord and thanked Him for His victory became known as the Valley of Blessing. Notice that the Valley of Blessing didn't occur after the battle was won. The people began to praise God and thank him for the victory as they marched into the battle. It is easy to praise God and thank Him after the battle has been won. Yet it's harder to praise God when the sickness hasn't gone away, your son is still in a state of rebellion, a marriage is still in distress. In times like theses we must find our Valley of Blessing. We can find it by praising God as we are marching into it and as we are in the thick of it. In the midst of the battle, go to this valley and praise the Lord. Sing to Him and thank Him for all the blessings in your life. Find your Valley of Blessing.

Vengeance Is Mine

If the battle is the Lord's, then vengeance is as well. Because of covenant, He will take vengeance on those who have wrongly hurt His people. The Lord will exact revenge on those who have caused unjust suffering and pain in our lives. Because of covenant, we can rest assured that one day, though it may not be immediate, Jesus will hold all accountable for their words and actions.

Words pierce like a sword and hurt just as much as a stress fracture or broken bone. Abusive words tear at the spirit and can have long-term effects. The children of God are clearly warned how powerful our words are. Observe Ephesians 4:29–32 in the New Living Translation.

> Don't use foul or abusive language. Let everything you say be good and helpful, so that your words will be an encouragement to those

who hear them. And do not bring sorrow to God's Holy Spirit by the way you live. Remember, he is the one who has identified you as his own, guaranteed that you will be saved on the day of redemption. Get rid of all bitterness, rage, anger, harsh words and slander, as well as all types of malicious behavior. Instead be kind to each other, tenderhearted, forgiving one another just as God through Christ has forgiven you.

The King James Version begins by saying, "Let no corrupt communication proceed out of your mouth." Corrupt words hurt others. Corrupt words do not minister grace to the hearer. They tear down and manipulate others. The Greek word for *corrupt* is *sapros*, meaning bad, rotten, decayed, and unwholesome—anything that sparks dissension or promotes division. A home will not be effective when it is divided by careless words. A home cannot stand if division arises from within. Satan's ultimate goal is to divide the home, to tear it apart, to cause division between husband and wife, parents and children—because if he can destroy the home, he can then affect every other area of our lives.

Through our choice of words, we have the opportunity to build up our families or tear them down. By choosing to build up others with our words we are speaking life into them. Ask the Holy Spirit to put a door on your lips and allow Him to open and close it. Proverbs 15:4 NIV says, "The tongue that brings healing is a tree of life, but a deceitful tongue crushes the spirit." Many people pierced by words are walking around with open wounds in need of the ultimate healer, Jesus Christ. As our covenant partner, Jesus wants to bandage what others have torn apart.

We are told as Christians not to return evil for evil. While this may go against everything we are feeling, we must trust our covenant partner, who commands us to "never pay back evil for evil to anyone," but rather to "respect what is right in the sight of all men. If possible, so far as it depends on you, be at peace with all men. Never take your own revenge, beloved, but leave room for the wrath of God, for it is written, 'Vengeance is Mine, I will repay,' says the Lord. 'But if your enemy is hungry, feed him, and if your enemy is thirsty, give him a drink; for in so doing you will heap burning coals upon his head.' Do not be overcome by evil, but overcome evil with good" (Rom. 12:17-21 NASB).

How do we overcome evil with good? To prevent evil from overcoming us, we must learn to forgive. Forgiveness is really for ourselves more than for those who have hurt us. Jesus commands every believer to walk in forgiveness. There are times when we do not feel like forgiving, but we are called to rise above our feelings, to forgive, and then let our feelings catch up with our choice. God honors those who honor Him, and by choosing to honor Him, we can reach total forgiveness. It will not be easy; it may be among the hardest things we will ever have to do, but it will prove to be the best thing for us mentally, spiritually and physically.

Someone once said, "Unforgiveness is like drinking poison and expecting the other person to die." So you ask, "I'll forgive, but can I grit my teeth while doing it? Is forgiveness a free pass for others to walk all over me?"

We know it is not. Remember that our covenant partner knows what has happened to us. Scripture teaches us why it is best for us to walk in forgiveness:

- "Bear with each other and forgive whatever grievances you may have against one another. Forgive as the Lord forgave you" (Col. 3:13 NIV).

- "Be kind and compassionate to one another, forgiving each other, just as in Christ God forgave you" (Eph. 4:32 NIV).
- "Forgive us our sins, for we also forgive everyone who sins against us. And lead us not into temptation" (Luke 11:4 NIV).
- "For if you forgive men when they sin against you, your heavenly Father will also forgive you. But if you do not forgive men their sins, your Father will not forgive your sins" (Matt. 6:14–15 NIV).
- "And when you stand praying, if you hold anything against anyone, forgive him, so that your Father in heaven may forgive your sins" (Mark 11:25 NIV).
- "This is how my heavenly Father will treat each of you unless you forgive your brother from your heart" (Matt. 18:35 NIV).

Notice how forgiveness toward offenders is directly related to how God forgives us. That is a thought worth pondering, for God conditions his forgiveness of us on our forgiveness of others.

A man named General Thorpe once said to John Wesley: "I never forgive and I never forget!" To which John Wesley replied: "Then, sir, I hope you never sin." Jesus says we must forgive from our hearts. How do we know if we have truly forgiven? How do we know if unforgiveness, which turns to anger, which turns to bitterness, is lodged in our hearts? If we allow ourselves to get to this point, we are in trouble. In his book *Total Forgiveness*, R. T. Kendall writes about a problem he encountered as a pastor and how he had to let go of a grudge that he had carried around for months.

I began to notice an interesting cycle: When I allowed the spirit of total forgiveness to reign in my heart, the peace would return; but when I would dwell with resentment on the likelihood that they wouldn't get caught, the peace would leave. I had to make an important decision: Which do I prefer—the peace or the bitterness? I couldn't have it both ways. I began to see that I was the one who was losing by nursing my attitude of unforgiveness. My bitterness wasn't damaging anyone but myself.[23]

According to Kendall, when we hold a grudge and feel like it is our responsibility to punish those who have wronged us, we grieve the Holy Spirit. Remember the song "This little light of mine, I'm going to let it shine"? The Holy Spirit is like a light inside of us. Grieving the Holy Spirit is like pouring water on a fire. When sin dampens our awareness of the Holy Spirit, we can lose our sense of peace. Kendall says that the "primary way we grieve the Spirit in our lives is by fostering bitterness in our hearts." He notes that in Ephesians 4:30–32 NIV, where the apostle Paul writes about grieving the Holy Spirit, the first thing mentioned is bitterness.

And do not grieve the Holy Spirit of God with whom you were sealed for the day redemption. Get rid of all bitterness, rage and anger, brawling and slander, along with every form of malice. Be kind and compassionate to one another, forgiving each other, just as Christ God forgave you.

---

23   R.T. Kendall, *Total Forgiveness* (Lake Mary, Florida 32746: Charisma House, 2002), Page XXVII.

Kendall writes: "What matters is that the Holy Spirit is able to dwell in us ungrieved, able to be utterly Himself. The degree to which the Holy Spirit is Himself in me will be the degree to which I am like Jesus and carry out His teachings."[24]

After reading this, I realized how much my unforgiveness hinders my relationship with God. It is a roadblock in my Christian walk. Once we are hurt, a huge hole opens in our hearts through which we seem to sink deeper and deeper. How do we begin to climb out of the hole? Every time we rehash the hurt that was done to us, we lodge it deeper and deeper into our hearts.[25] We know that Scripture says, "Out of the overflow of the heart the mouth speaks." What we are upset about, angry about, or bitter about will eventually come out of our mouths and we will hurt others. We don't want to get caught in a vicious cycle, hurting others because we are hurt.

We must make a conscious choice every day to forgive. It is not easy, but if we are searching for peace, God will help us. We may think it is absolutely impossible to forgive a cheating wife, a verbally abusive husband, a physically abusive parent, or a sexually abusive relative. The pain may feel too deep. Yet God is faithful in helping us accomplish His will.

Research suggests that unforgiveness can affect us physically. In her book *Who Switched Off My Brain?* Dr. Caroline Leaf says that every thought we have creates a corresponding electrochemical reaction in the brain. Different chemicals are released when we are happy and when we are sad, afraid, and angry. She says,

24   Kendall, page XXXIII.
25   Kendall, page XXXIII.

Our brains can be compared to a prolific factory producing a variety of chemicals depending on what type of emotion you are experiencing. Depending on whether or not these emotions are toxic to your body, the chemicals will either help you or harm you. If they are harmful they create conditions for a host of health problems that will manifest in both the body and the mind. Emotions that regularly release a torrent of destructive chemicals that will be the most damaging over time are: unforgiveness, anger, rage, resentment, depression, worry, anxiety, frustration, fear, excessive grief and guilt.

Research shows that around 87% of illnesses can be attributed to our thought life, and approximately 13% to diet, genetics and environment. Studies conclusively link more chronic diseases (also known as lifestyle diseases) to an epidemic of toxic emotions in our culture.[26]

According to Leaf, there are two important groups of emotions: positive, faith-based emotions and negative, fear-based emotions. She says faith and fear are not just emotions, but spiritual forces with chemical and electrical representation in the body. Consequently they directly affect bodily function.

Every emotion results in an attitude. An attitude is a state of mind that produces a reaction in the body and results in behavior. All negative emotions, Leaf says, result from fear, and all positive emotions evolve out of faith. She lists as examples

26   Dr. Caroline Leaf, *Who Switched off MY BRAIN?* (Dallas, TX 75244: Switch on Your Brain USA Inc., 2008), Page 4.

of faith-based emotions love, joy, peace, happiness, kindness, gentleness, self-control, forgiveness, and patience. These produce good attitudes. Examples of fear-based emotions are hate, worry, anxiety, anger, hostility, rage, ill will, resentment, frustration, impatience, and irritation. These produce toxic attitudes, which produce toxic responses in the body.

Leaf says that one of the most powerful of the fear-based emotions is hate, which goes hand-in-hand with bitterness, resentment, and anger—all the emotions that arise when we hold unforgiveness in our hearts. The root of unforgiveness turns to bitterness, resentment, and anger, leading us to hate.

Leaf says that emotions such as hate take up physical space in our brains and grow like weeds, eventually covering up everything else. "When hate is allowed all that space, it integrates and eventually takes control of the magic trees (nerve cells) of the mind and insidiously affects all your thoughts and emotions," Leaf says. And "the only way to deal with toxic symptoms that plague our hearts or to prevent them altogether is to start dealing with repressed unforgiveness, anger, rage, hatred or whatever other form of toxic thoughts are taking over the mind."[27]

She points out that we can bury our emotions, but we must remember that we are burying something that lives and that the mind perceives suppressed emotions as fear. Forgiveness is the sixth step of Leaf's brain-detoxing program. She says forgiveness is a choice, an act of the free will that allows us to release all the toxic thoughts of anger, resentment, bitterness, shame, grief, regret, guilt, and hate. Her research indicates that as long as unhealthy toxic thoughts dominate the mind, new healthy thoughts and memories cannot grow. Leaf points

---

27   Leaf, page 21.

to the results of a "forgiveness study" by researchers at the University of Wisconsin which found that those who develop an ability to forgive have greater control over their emotions and are significantly less angry, upset, and hurt, and consequently much healthier.

Kendall writes: "The ultimate proof of total forgiveness takes place when we sincerely petition the Father to let those who have hurt us off the hook—even if they have hurt not only us, but also those close to us."[28]

True Forgiveness Holds No Wrongs

Have you forgiven but not forgotten? True biblical forgiveness involves both. While I realize we cannot program our minds to erase a memory, especially a bad one, we can ask God to cleanse our minds of negative thoughts about a hurtful person or situation. We can ask the Holy Spirit to help us walk in forgiveness so that the thought or presence of this person will not stir up painful feelings. We have forgiven, so we must give those who have offended us over to God, our covenant partner, to do with as He pleases. God is a just God and will take His wrath as He desires.

How does God forgive our sins? "I will forgive their wickedness, and I and will never again remember their sins" (Jer. 31:34 NLT).

The Hebrew root for *remember* is *zakar*, which means to recall, think of, mention, or record.[29] God says He will forget our sins

---

28   Kendall, page 4.
29   Bible Study Tools, "Zakar," The KJV Old Testament Hebrew Lexicon, http://www.biblestudytools.com/lexicons/hebrew/kjv/zakar.html (accessed June 28, 2012).

and will not think of them or mention them to us. In other words, God will not hold our sins against us. Yes, we can face consequences for our sins, but if we confess our sins He is faithful and just to forgive our sins and cleanse us off all our unrighteousness. If we are washed in the blood of Jesus, our sins are washed away with that blood.

God's forgiveness keeps no record of wrongs. If Jesus is our model of forgiveness then we must choose to forgive others as God forgives us. We must strive not to hold a wrong over or against the one who hurt us. It is so much easier to dwell on the past, but as hard as it is, we must give the past over to God. God knows our hurts, and as our covenant partner He will hold all accountable for their actions one day. Kendall says, "It is a demonstration of greater grace when we are fully aware of what occurred—and we still choose to forgive."[30] Scripture says, "Love keeps no record of wrongs" (1 Cor. 13:5 NIV).

I am a list-maker. I make a list for work, a list for personal to-dos, a grocery list, a house list, a yard list. I write everything down. I seem to have a poor short-term memory, so I have to jot things down a lot. I am ashamed to admit this, but once I was tempted to write down what my family members had said to me that hurt my feelings terribly. When the situation came up again, I wanted to remind them how badly they had hurt me. Reading Kendall's book, I heard God say, "Tear it up." Tear up my list of wrongs.

Whether our list is written on paper or stored in our memories, we must tear it up. In doing so, we are freeing up space in our brains. Kendall writes, "Total forgiveness obviously sees the evil but chooses to erase it. Before a grudge becomes

---

30   Kendall page 18,

lodged in the heart, the offense must be willfully forgotten. Resentment must not be given an opportunity to set in. The love in 1 Corinthians 13 (which is referred to as the love chapter in the Bible) can only come by following a lifestyle of total forgiveness."[31]

Biblical forgiveness also doesn't say, " I'll forgive, but I've got a right to be mad. And there's no telling how long I'll be mad." Jesus said be angry but do not sin. Anger is a God-given emotion. It should propel us to a righteous action. But it is that action that determines if we sin or not. If we stay mad because we think it will cause an enemy to suffer, we must remember that Jesus said not to return evil for evil. He said, "Vengeance is Mine; I will repay" those who have hurt you. When we choose forgiveness, we are taking someone who has offended us off our hook and placing him onto God's. We can trust our covenant partner to deal justly with that person. Kendall says, "Confidence toward God is ultimately what total forgiveness is all about; He is the one I want to please at the end of the day."[32]

In the past, I would rehearse what to say the next time I saw my antagonist, just to let that person know I was still angry. I would walk through conversations in my mind. I prepared answers. I was ready to reply to certain questions in case they came up. I wanted to tell the person how angry I was, how I was suffering and in agony over what was said to me, or how I was treated.
But we must forgive on a daily basis. Kendall writes about showing grace and mercy at the same time. He says, "Graciousness is shown by what you don't say, even if what

31   Kendall page 126.
32   Kendall, page 18

you could say would be true."[33] To act graciously toward our offender is a concept hard to grasp. Scripture says that Jesus' lips are anointed with grace. I remember praying, "Lord, anoint my lips with grace right now before I say something I'm going to regret." God, as our covenant partner, will take action in His own time against those who have hurt us. "Never pay back evil for evil to anyone. Do things in such a way that everyone can see you are honorable. Do your part to live in peace with everyone, as much as possible" (Rom. 12:17–18 NLT).

If we try to take our own vengeance, we are getting in God's way. God is fully capable of handling our situation on His own.

> Dear friends, never avenge yourselves. Leave that to God. For it is written, "I will take vengeance; I will repay those who deserve it," says the Lord. Instead, do what the Scriptures say: "If your enemies are hungry, feed them. If they are thirsty, give them something to drink, and they will be ashamed of what they have done to you." Don't let evil get the best of you, but conquer evil by doing good.
> —Rom. 12:19–21 NLT

There it is: conquer evil by doing good. As hard as it may be, we must leave revenge up to our covenant partner, Jesus. Our part of being in covenant with Jesus is to allow Him to do justice. He is a just God, and we must trust that He will bring justice to our situation.

---

33   Kendall, page 126

Biblical forgiveness doesn't say, "I'll forgive, but things will never be the same between us." As Christians, we must develop a forgiveness that is biblical. We need to know what to do with our emotions. In addition, we must show our children how to handle their anger so they can avoid unforgiveness and bitterness.

To keep ourselves from bitterness, we must acknowledge our anger, pray for God to help us control our emotions, pray for Him to bless our enemies, and give them over to God so we will not return evil for evil. But what happens next? What happens to the relationship after we forgive?

If we want to stay biblical, we must go as far as possible to restore the relationship to normal. I am not saying that if a person broke our trust we must trust him again. If the person is not repentant or does not change, we should not put ourselves in harm's way. However, if we are going to reach complete forgiveness, there is a restoration process. This is the hardest part. It is easier to forgive if we do not have to see the person again. But the people we are closest to and have relationships with are the most likely to hurt us.

Why is restoration a biblical issue? While we were still sinners, God in Christ was reconciling the world unto Himself. And after we receive Jesus as our Lord and Savior, we are placed in a right standing with Him, and we remain there. Yes, we will mess up; we will sin; we will hurt other people. But God, in His mercy, will forgive us and keep us in a right standing with Him. By no means is this an invitation to sin. It does, however, indicate how we are to treat others.

How does reconciliation begin? Prayer is a good place to start. Reconciliation can be a process. God honors those who honor Him, and He is in the business of doing miracles. He will give us the strength to mend fences and bridge the gap. With the help of God Almighty, we can achieve true forgiveness. No one may understand the strength it takes to truly forgive, but God calls His children to forgiveness and He will make it possible for our hearts to be whole again.

Crying out for a place to be truly known and loved, the blind songwriter Ken Medema wrote the following:

> If this is not a place where tears are understood,
> then where shall I go to cry?
> And if this is not a place where my spirit can take wings,
> then where shall I go to fly?
> I don't need another place for tryin' to impress you
> with just how good and virtuous I am.
> No, no, no
> I don't need another place for always bein' on top of things.
> Everybody knows that it's a sham, it's a sham.
> I don't need another place for always wearin' smiles
> even when it's not the way I feel.
> I don't need another place to mouth the old platitudes.
> Everybody knows that it's not real.
> So if this is not a place where my questions can be asked,
> then where shall I go to seek?
> And if this is not a place where my heart cry can be heard,
> where, tell me where, shall I go to speak?[34]

---

34   Ken Medema, "If This Is Not a Place," Ken Medema's 25 to Life: For Prisoners of Hope Everywhere, February 28, 1997, Brier Patch Music, Audio C.D.

What is your image of God- the picture you have of Him in your mind? This alone will determine if he is your safe place or not. Do you feel safe to be real, to share your heart, or be vulnerable? If we see God as a parent whose approval we will never gain, a teacher whose test we will never pass or a manager who expects more than we could ever give, then we will never view God as our safe place. In order to truly forgive I believe sharing our heart with God will help us reach total forgiveness. Scripture says we can boldly approach the throne room of grace and God will give us mercy to help us in our time of need (Heb. 4:14-16 NIV).

My experience has been that the people who hurt us are often unaware of what they have done. They are enjoying life and moving forward, while we are throwing our own pity party, seeking sympathy from anyone and everyone who will listen. It can be therapeutic to tell a close friend whom we know will keep our conversation in confidence. However, we must evaluate our motive. Most of the time, I have found myself wanting to "confide" in a friend so I can discredit, damage, or ruin someone's credibility, character, or reputation. If the person we confide in will never look at the other person the same way again, then we should talk only to God. We do not want to sin against our offender by gossiping. God invites us to freely come to him. As our covenant partner he is always there ready to listen.

Total forgiveness must take place in our hearts. If we have truly forgiven, we can be around our offender and not be affected. Our mouths are first to prove if we have totally forgiven.

Forgiveness is about our freedom as Christians. God commands us to forgive because if we don't, our hearts will never heal. God wants us to be whole and healthy so we may be clean vessels for His Spirit to work through. As Christians, we are His workmanship, created in Christ Jesus to do good. God has good works in mind for us. I want to join Him in His activity. I want to be a part of His plan of redemption for a lost world. Let us find our place in that plan. Because of covenant, we stand clean and forgiven before a holy God. May God soften our hearts and help us to extend His forgiveness to others as well.

chapter 5

COVENANT FRIENDSHIP

> And the scripture was fulfilled that says, "Abraham believed God and it was credited to him as righteousness," and he was called God's friend.
>
> —James 2:23 NIV

It is difficult to imagine that God could be a friend with a human being. When I think of God's holiness and my sinful nature, it is hard to comprehend that God would enter into such a relationship. What a privilege it must have been for the God of the universe to say, "Abraham, you are My friend."

Most people choose friends carefully. Most friendships develop between people who think alike, believe alike, and want similar things in life. They usually have much in common.

Friendships are usually intentional. They are proactive, not reactive. Both parties must put forth effort to maintain the relationship. Friendships shape and even prolong lives. The Bible says that a friend loves at all times and that if we want friends, we must be friendly. Friends, who love at all times laugh at jokes when they are not funny, keep your dog even though they don't want to, and celebrate birthdays and anniversaries. A friend will cry with you when you don't have the words to explain why you are crying. A friend will listen even when he does not have the time. Friendships are work, and having friends is worth the effort.

Solomon was considered the wisest man on earth; God blessed him with wisdom to lead His people. Job was the most patient man of all time; he persevered through pain and loss. Nehemiah risked his life to do God's work of rebuilding the fallen walls of Jerusalem. Jeremiah was God's weeping prophet, who felt God's heart for His people; Isaiah's lips were anointed with a burning coal to purify his words about a coming savior. David was the apple of God's eye. Amos was a man who stood for God's justice. But God declared Abraham alone His friend. What does it take to be a friend of God?

In Genesis 18, we are told that Abraham was sitting outside his tent when he saw three men walking toward him. Bible scholars believe one of these men was God and the other two were angels. Abraham recognized that these were not ordinary men. He knew immediately that the Lord was approaching, and he ran out to greet Him.

Abraham fell to his knees and said, "If I have found favor in your eyes, do not pass your servant by." He invited the three to stay for dinner and ran back to the tent to tell Sarah, his wife, to start cooking—and only the best. The Lord was coming to dine with His friend.

I believe God approaches us many times in life. We know Jesus chases after our hearts. When we allow Him to be our

Lord and Savior, we are sealed for eternity. But He continues to ask us to open every door of our lives. He seeks entrance to every area. In Revelation 3:20 NIV, Jesus says, "Here I Am! I stand at the door and knock. If anyone hears My voice and opens the door, I will come in and eat with him, and he with Me." Is there a door that you have not opened to Christ? What kind of dinner are you preparing for Him? Only the best like Abraham, who gave the first fruits of his labor?

Abraham's actions showed that he put God first in his life. What position does God hold with us? Is He at the center of everything we do and say? Does every decision we make revolve around our relationship with the Savior?

It is scary to let go and allow God into places we feel we can control on our own. Maybe it is managing our finances, letting go of a sinful habit, controlling our temper, or putting a lid on gossip. Does Jesus want us to pursue purity, wait for God's timing, or put away our pride? What door is God asking us to open so that He can assist us?

In a basketball game, an assist occurs when a player helps a teammate score. God wants to assist us in accomplishing the goals He has for us. That requires allowing Him into every area of our lives. Here is how Jesus says He will uphold us:

> But you Israel, My servant, Jacob whom I have chosen, you descendants of Abraham my friend. I took you from the ends of the earth; from its farthest corners I called you. I said, "You are my servant"; I have chosen you and have not rejected you. So do not fear, for I am with you; do not be dismayed, for I am your God. I

will strengthen you and help you; I will uphold
you with My righteous right hand.

—Isa. 41:8–10 NIV

In Exodus 17, we see how the Israelites experienced an unexpected attack by the Amalekites. Amalek was the son of Eliphaz, Esau's eldest son. The Amalekites were distant cousins. They probably held a grudge because they saw God's hand on Israel as He protected the Jews on their journey to the Promised Land. The Israelites were walking under God's covenant, and He met their needs with manna from heaven and water from a rock.

Did the Amalekites attack Israel because they witnessed blessings that God gives only to His people? Did they realize that the blessings promised through the birthright of Jacob were now coming to the Israelites and not to them?

Battles come our way every day. Some last longer than others. The Amalekites were Israel's persistent and unremitting enemy. The Amalekites blocked Israel's way into the Promised Land (Ex. 17:8–16). The Amalekites joined forces with the Midianites and beleaguered the Israelites in Gideon's day (Judg. 6:3). It was an Amalekite who killed King Saul (1 Sam. 15:9, 28). The Amalekites continually sought to hinder the progress of God's people and rob them of His blessings.

For Christians, sin can be an unrelenting enemy. Sin robs us of God's blessing in our lives. Sin pulls us away from God. It hinders our spiritual walk and erodes our joy. It gives us a divided heart. It controls us with habits we cannot give up and keep yielding to. It entangles us in a web that we have woven by our own choices.

Our own selfish nature, the flesh, can also rob us of God's blessings. The flesh and the Holy Spirit will always be at war. The Holy Spirit fights for our minds because as man thinks, so he is. What we believe will be in direct correlation to how we act and react. What we believe to be true about ourselves, others, and the way God thinks about us will play out in our daily lives. Paul said we are to put on the mind of Christ Jesus.

Yet another adversary hunts us like a roaring lion. We are not always fighting against ourselves, but Satan himself. He wants to see us defeated. We may not always realize that he is the one attacking us. But the battle has already been won. The day Jesus died on the cross, Satan's future was determined. But the Bible warns us we must still put on our armor and fight back. "For we wrestle not against flesh and blood, but against principalities, against powers, against the rulers of the darkness of this world, against spiritual wickedness in high places" (Eph. 6:12 KJV).

It is easy to identify the Amalekites in our lives. Mine are persistent! Yet the battle is the Lord's. We serve a God who calls Himself the great I AM!

When Moses first encountered his God in the burning bush, he had so much to learn. It was a day-by-day process, and he was scared. He told God to find someone else to lead His people into the Promised Land. Did he doubt God or did he doubt himself? God asked Moses to lead His people out of captivity, out from beneath the most powerful nation in the world. God pointed out the path and said, "Go, and I will be with you. I will be with you every step of the way. When you fall down, I will come and get you. If you need miraculous signs and wonders, I will provide them. If you need encouragement,

I will send others into your life to uphold you. If you need strength, I will be your source. Now go!"

What does this have to do with friendship? We take advice only from those we respect and trust, those we know quite well. God promises He will lead us and guide us in the right direction, and He does not disappoint. "The Lord will guide you always, the Lord will meet all your needs in a sun-scorched land and strengthen your frame. You will be like a well-watered garden and a spring whose water never fails" (Isa. 58:11 NIV).

The Amalekites moved to attack the Israelites at Rephidim, a place of rest and relaxation. Just when we think we are in a place of comfort and rest, we see another battle on the horizon. The Israelites had witnessed water flowing from a rock. They had seen the hand of God and His provision for them. God was on their side, providing for them each day, but still the enemy came.

Moses told Joshua to choose men and prepare to fight the Amalekites. There were thousands of men to choose from, but Joshua was told to select a few. What kind of person would we choose to fight alongside us? Do we have friends who would go with us to battle?

I'm sure Joshua chose godly men, men who had a relationship with the living God, men who got on their knees and cried out to God because they believed in prayer. Those are the type of friends I long for.

The night before I was to have surgery, I called certain friends I knew would pray for me. I was scared. I felt helpless, unsure of the unknown. I called friends I knew would lift me up to

God and ask Him to guide the doctor's hands and mind. I called friends I knew would continue to pray for my healing afterward.

When we enter into covenant with Jesus, we gain a faithful friend, a friend for life. Toward the end of His life on earth, Jesus told His disciples they were more than just His servants; they were His friends. "I no longer call you servants, because a master doesn't confide in his servants. Now you are My friends, since I have told you everything the Father has told Me" (John 15:15 NLT). This shared knowledge of the Father allowed Jesus and His disciples to connect on a deeper level of friendship.

By God's very nature, He is a friend to us. He sent His Son to die a brutal death on a cross in order to have a relationship with us. God loves each of us with a perfect love. He wants and knows what is best for us. He loves us enough to discipline us. He will never forsake us. He is the prefect friend.

Jesus said the greatest commandment is to love the Lord with all our hearts, all our minds, and all our souls. God loves with a perfect love; therefore, he is a perfect friend. This is a love worth seeking and this is a friendship worth pursuing. God does not hide from those who seek Him with whole hearts. Ask God to give you a desire to know Him more.

> This Highest Priest of ours [Jesus] understands our weaknesses, for He faced all of the same temptations we do, yet He did not sin. So let us come boldly to the throne of our gracious God. There we will receive His mercy, and we will find grace to help us when we need it.
> —Heb. 4:15–16 NLT

Another translation says we do not have a High Priest who cannot sympathize with our weaknesses. Jesus as our High Priest experienced every form of temptation. There is nothing we go through that He cannot understand. This is true friendship. Most people want to be understood. Jesus understands and will stay close to us through our trials and temptations, helping us through them. It is impossible not to have trials and temptations, but we have an advocate who not only will be with us when we need Him, but also will understand the situation perfectly. "For Christ has entered into heaven itself to appear now before God as our Advocate" (Heb. 9:24 NLT).

Why is Facebook so popular? Isn't it because each of us has a desire to connect to others, to know and be known? In their book *The Relationship Edge,* Jerry Acuff and Wally Wood list thirteen traits that they say are common to all people:
1. In general, people have a desire to be important.
2. They want to be appreciated.
3. They are not nearly as interested in you, your interest, or your concerns as they are in themselves.
4. Most people want two things out of life: success and happiness.
5. They want you to listen to them with your full attention.
6. People will connect with you only if they feel you sincerely value them.
7. Most people make decisions emotionally and defend them logically.
8. The average person's attention span is very short.
9. People with common interest have natural rapport.
10. People want to be understood.

11. People are drawn to people who are genuinely interested in them.
12. Most people love to teach.
13. People want to associate with others who they believe can help them in some aspect of their lives.[35]

In *How to Win Friends and Influence People*, Dale Carnegie wrote: "You can make more friends in two months by being interested in other people than you can in two years by trying to get other people interested in you."[36] We have a God-given desire to be fully known and loved. We can become the friends Jesus created us to be if we stay connected to Him. We can love with a love we could never attain on our own if we remain in touch with Jesus.

> I am the true vine, and My Father is the gardener. He cuts off every branch that doesn't produce fruit, and He prunes the branches that do bear fruit so they will produce even more. You have already been pruned for greater fruitfulness by the message I have given you. Remain in me and I will remain in you. For a branch cannot produce fruit if it is severed from the vine, and you cannot be fruitful apart from Me. Yes, I am the vine; you are the branches. Those who remain in Me, and I in them, will produce much fruit. For apart from Me you can do nothing.
>
> —John 15:1-5 NLT

---

35   Jerry Acuff and Wally Wood, The Relationship Edge (Hoboken, New Jersey: John Wiley & Sons, Inc., 2007), pages 55-56.

36   Dale Carnegie, "The Quotation Page, "Michael Moncur, (accessed June 28, 2012).

Fruitful relationships will blossom for the kingdom of God when we stay connected to Jesus and abide in Him. Stay in His word. Remain in prayer. Talk often about what He is doing in your life. Talk to your children over and over about the faithfulness of God. Fruitful relationships overflow from our relationship with Jesus. If we stay connected to Him, He will give us a genuine love and concern for others. God will call us to be His hands and His feet, to witness to others what His friendship is like.

Joshua picked a few men to fight with him. Would you consider yourself worthy to go into battle with one of your friends? When we stay connected with Jesus, others will want to be around us. Others will want us by their side in the tough going.

Moses told Joshua that he, Aaron, and Hur would go up to the top of a hill where they could view the battle. Moses brought God's staff, which represented His power, and held it up high. When he did, Joshua and the Israelites prevailed, but when Moses lowered the staff the Amalekites prevailed. Imagine the sweat that ran down his brow. His arms grew tired; his muscles cramped. Finally, his arms became too weary to hold the staff aloft, so Aaron and Hur found a stone on which Moses could sit. They sat on each side and held up his arms. The Bible says that they did this until sunset, when the battle was won. On that spot, Moses built an altar and called it *Yahweh Nissi*, The Lord Is My Banner (Ex. 17:15 NIV).

How is this a story about friendship? Look at the key players: Moses, Joshua and his men, Aaron and Hur. Each played an important part; each made a difference in the lives of the others.

One of my dear friends called me crying because she had broken her kneecap in a skiing accident. She was bound to the couch for eight weeks. At first her spirits were high and she was optimistic about the healing process. But then, as she lay on the couch with her knee propped up, unable to go to the grocery store and get food, unable to drive to work, unable to move without hurting, she realized how much she needed other people.

Why had God allowed this to happen she wondered? Deep down she knew there was a reason. She told me she was extremely independent and did not rely on others. However, she said, if there was ever a time she needed a friend, it was now. "It's not when I'm on top of the mountain that I need people," she said. "It's now, when I'm stuck in the valley." She needed a Moses to intercede for her healing. She needed a Joshua to fight with her. She needed Aaron and Hur to come alongside of her and hold her up.

But where are Moses, Joshua, Aaron, and Hur when we need them? You may be the one in need, or perhaps God has placed someone in your path that He wants you to pray for, encourage, help financially, make dinner for, or listen to. We must stand up with our brothers and sisters against the Amalekites in our lives.

Furthermore, an Amalekite lurks in each of us. We deal with a selfish flesh that wages war against the Holy Spirit's work. God has declared war on the flesh and will put to death any area not subjected to His authority or under His banner. Jesus fights for His children and sits at the right hand of the Father interceding for us. God watches over each breath we take. Jesus said that in this world we will have tribulation, but we are not to worry because He has overcome the world. As children of the Most High King, we will see, touch, and taste His victory. How wonderful that God allows us to be part of something so much bigger than our problems. "We will shout for joy when you are victorious and will lift up our banners in the name of our God. May the Lord grant all your requests" (Ps. 20:5 NIV).

Moses and Joshua acknowledged their need for God as well as for other people in their lives. Both knew they were not fighting alone. Both had a conscious dependence on the Lord.

Many times I allow fear to overtake my mind and control my thoughts. I realize I am paralyzed; I avoid a certain task, fearing the outcome. I find myself avoiding certain people in fear of rejection. It helps, at those times, to remind myself that God is with me. I may fail and experience rejection, yet God is not only with me, but also as my covenant partner he goes before me.

The battle is ultimately for our thoughts, which dictate our actions. If I allow myself to give in to fear, then my day will be full of fear-based emotions such as worry, doubt, anxiety and distress. It's easy to lose focus of controlling our thoughts or even identifying negative ones. And it takes faith to believe God when he says; "I am with you always, even to the end of the age" (Matt. 28:20 NLT). But faith is what pushes us forward leaving the negative emotions behind. Faith believes that God has summoned you by name and called you for a purpose. It takes faith to daily trust your covenant partner to give you the courage to do what He has called you to do. Dale Carnegie wrote: "Most of the important things in the world have been accomplished by people who have kept on trying when there seemed to be no hope at all."[37] We must not allow fear to control our actions but allow Christ to point us in the direction He wants us to go. As Christians our hope is in Jesus Christ who is the anchor of our soul. It's sounds cliché' but it is not as important how we start our Christian walk as it is how we finish it.

"See then that you walk circumspectly, not as fools but as wise, redeeming the time because the days are evil" (Eph. 5:15–16 NKJV). Time can be my worst enemy. The enemy can easily distract me from doing what I know God has called me to do. Not managing our time appropriately can cause us to lose a conscience dependence on the Lord. We must redeem the time the Lord has given each one of us.

As Moses stood on top of the Mountain with Aaron and Hur on each side of him he was then physically secure yet mentally was the battle still raging?

What was on Moses' mind while he was on top of the hill holding up the rod of God? Was he praying for victory as he looked down and saw Joshua and his troops battling the enemy? Once Moses had his friends there to hold his arms up could he now begin to pray for others strength verses his own?

After fighting his own spiritual battle and receiving strength from his friends, he could now lift up each and every man unto the Lord in prayer. His battle in the spiritual realm was just as important as the physical one taking place down below. Praying to God on another's behalf is called intercession. One study Bible defines *intercession* as "holy, believing, persevering

---

37   Dale Carnegie, "Dale Carnegie Quotes," ThinkExit.com, Quotations, http://www.thinkexit.com/quotations/most_of_the_important_things_in_ the_world_have_/10564.html (accessed June 28, 2012).

prayer whereby someone pleads with God on behalf of another or others who desperately need God's intervention." The men below definitely needed God's intervention. Maybe God sent Moses friends to carry him physically so Moses could be free mentally to pray for victory below.

Intercession is said to be a spiritual discipline. God will place burdens on our hearts for those whom we must lift up to Him in prayer. In these situations we must be sensitive to the Holy Spirit's prompting.

As believers, we are called to pray for others. Moses knew he could not fight physically; in fact he was almost worn out physically until his friends came along, but he knew he could fight spiritually. You and I may be miles apart from friends and family, but still we can lift them up to the Lord in prayer. I could not visit my friend with the broken kneecap, but I could lift her up to the Lord. Search for Scripture verses that call us to a life of intercession for those whom God has placed on our hearts. It may not be a specific person or persons, but a community, a state, or a nation. If we align our hearts with God, the cry of our hearts will be the cry of God's heart. For what and for whom do you feel God tugging you to pray?

On September 11, 2007, I got up and went through my usual routine. As I was pouring myself a cup of coffee, the Lord's presence overwhelmed me. I suddenly felt an urge to be alone and get into the Word. I opened my Bible to 2 Chronicles 14 and began reading about King Asa, who once brought peace to a nation because he did what was pleasing and good in the sight of the Lord.

Asa commanded the people to seek the Lord and obey His commands. But even as he did well in the eyes of the Lord, an enemy attacked. Asa had 580,000 men; the enemy's army numbered one million. Asa deployed his men to battle and, as he did, he cried out to the Lord this prayer: "O Lord, no one but You can help the powerless against the mighty! Help us, O Lord our God, for we trust in You alone. It is in Your name that we have come against this vast horde. O Lord, you are God; do not let mere men prevail against You!" (2 Chron. 14:11 NLT).

As I read Asa's story, I was compelled to fast and pray all day for God to protect our nation. I got in my car to go to work. On the radio, I heard Nancy Lee Demas talking about the same Scripture. She was also calling prayer warriors to pray that day. What might have happened that day had God's people failed to pray? How many people had a burden to rise up our nation in prayer?

An Ethiopian army of a million men and three hundred chariots out numbered King Asa. He said no one but God could help the powerless against the mighty. Asa obeyed God and prayed. God chose to intervene in the lives of His people. We must pay close attention to the burdens God places on our hearts. How many promptings of God have I missed to pray for others, for my community, for our nation? Prayer takes place when God reaches out to His people and joins His heart to theirs. Only then can we see through God's eyes.

"I exhort first of all," Paul wrote to Timothy, "that supplications, prayers, intercessions, and giving of thanks be made for all men" (1 Tim. 2:1 NKJV).

Ephesians 6:18 NKJV tells us to be "praying always with all prayer and supplication in the Spirit, being watchful to this end with all perseverance and supplication for all the saints."

In Exodus 32, we see Moses climbing Mount Sinai to spend forty days alone with God. During that time, God showed Moses the wickedness in the hearts of His people. Moses saw the sin that caused them to practice idolatry. He had not so clearly known their desperate need for God, nor had he realized God's pending judgment until God revealed this to him. Suddenly Moses began to see the people as God did. His heart was moved with compassion for the people in their desperate condition.

Moses pleaded with God to save the people from their sin. He was so moved that he asked God if he could take their place. Moses was willing to sacrifice his life for the lives of the people who were, at that moment, at the foot of the mountain worshiping a golden calf. "Yet now, if You will forgive their sin—but if not, I pray, blot me out of Your book which You have written" (Ex. 32:32 NKJV).

Could you or I pray that prayer for our children, a spouse, or those who are closest to us?

Jesus' prayer life was marked by intercession for others. His prayer life was Spirit-led. He was in tune with the Holy Spirit's prompting when it was time to be alone with God. Look at the faithful prayer of Jesus in John 17. Jesus prayed to the Father for all who would become believers down through the ages. But He also prayed specifically for those whom God had entrusted to Him. Imagine what the Father revealed to Jesus about these men. Jesus knew their strengths, weaknesses, struggles, and temptations. He knew exactly how to pray for them. And we know He was obedient in doing so. Jesus' prayer began as a prayer for the world, but became a specific prayer for those who would reach the world on His behalf: Peter, the rock of the Church; John, whom He loved dearly; Andrew, who wasn't afraid to tell anyone of his Lord, and others.

Whom has God entrusted to your influence? Whom do you feel accountable for? Whom are you called to pray for? God has given us a variety of relationships—marriage partners, children, co-workers, friends, and our church family. How are we relating to these people?

"For the eyes of the Lord run to and fro throughout the whole earth, to show Himself strong on behalf of those whose heart is loyal to Him" (2 Chron. 16:9 NKJV). God will use a loyal heart committed to Him. Can you imagine God's eyes every morning scanning the entire earth looking for those who will be committed to Him for that day? God told Asa that He continually watches for those who are steadfast in their resolve for the Lord. God gave Asa victory over the Ethiopian army despite the odds he faced.

However, the next time Asa faced a relentless enemy, he failed to trust in God's strength. This opposing army was smaller than the one before, but it defeated him. Why would Asa's faith fail him after he had experienced such a tremendous earlier victory with the Lord?

Despite Asa's faltering faith, the Lord came alongside of the king and reminded him that the God of the universe never sleeps, never grows tired, and never stops searching for those whose hearts are committed to Him. The question is not whether God is looking for people to join Him in His work, but whether we are committed to Him. When God demonstrates His power in a believer's life, we see hearts changed—not only ours, but the hearts we have prayed for.

The Psalmist David said he had never seen the righteous forsaken. Our covenant partner, God Himself, will come alongside of us and help us hold up His banner, or He may send people into our lives to help us *to do so. Yahweh Nissi,* The Lord Is My Banner. Keep on asking, keep on looking, keep on knocking, and may the door of grace and mercy be opened to you.

chapter 6

COVENANT MATURING

Faith in Jesus Christ is a cognitive, passionate, and moral commitment to that which stands up under the scrutiny of the mind, the heart, and the conscience.[38]

—Ravi Zacharias

Isn't it amazing how fast children change and grow up? We hold them in our arms, rock them, sing them a lullaby, and when next we look up, they are running out the door with our car keys. At that point all we can do is pray. It is said that crawling is actually a critical developmental milestone with long-term benefits that we are only now beginning to recognize. Some doctors believe crawling is part of a child's healthy brain development. So the saying "You have to crawl before you can walk" is true.

Research suggests that crawling allows proper development of the brain and nervous system. A baby's brain is composed of millions of nerve cells called neurons, which are not yet

---

38   Ravi Zacharis, "tumblr. Follow the World's Creators," http://www.tumblr. com/tagged/ravi_zacharius?before=1297968007 (accessed July 1, 2012).

connected to each other. Science proposes that through the act of crawling these neurons begin to become stimulated as they connect to one another. It is believed that crawling not only helps develop hand/eye coordination but also has long-term benefits for other parts of the brain such as comprehension, concentration and memory. As the child analyzes their environment and determines where they want to go they are not only growing physically but mentally by developing their balance and space perception.

Our relationship with Jesus is called our Christian walk. As we walk through life with Jesus, we should mature spiritually. I can only hope that the older I get, the closer I am to God because of my knowledge and understanding of Him but this takes a lot of discipline.

Even though we often try to run before we can walk, it is comforting to know that God, as our covenant partner, is committed to our spiritual growth. Paul wrote: "Become mature, attaining to the whole measure of the fullness of Christ, then we will no longer be infants, tossed back and forth by the waves and blown here and there by every wind of teaching and by the cunning and craftiness of men in their deceitful scheming" (Eph. 4:13–14 NIV).

A lot in this world can blow us around like leaves in the wind. Paul is asking if we are sound in our doctrine so we can identify false teaching. As parents can we point out to our children what Scripture says is the truth verses what our culture says is truth? Have we spent enough time in God's Word to know how to make important personal decisions?

Jesus told His disciples that He had to go away so he could send the Holy Spirit. "But it is actually best for you that I go away, because if I don't, the Counselor won't come. If I do go away, He will come because I will send Him to you. And when He comes, He will convince the world of its sin, and of God's righteousness, and of the coming judgment" (John 16:7–8 NLT).

When you become a Christian, it is the Holy Spirit who convicts you of your sin and helps you see your need for a Savior. Before I was a Christian, I thought that I was a fairly good person. Yes, I made mistakes, but my life was back on track. Even so a feeling of guilt followed me everywhere I went. I felt jaded and tainted by my past decisions.

God surrounded me with amazing Christian friends and I began to learn. I was intrigued with their beliefs and standards for living. These friends convinced me that Jesus wanted to cleanse me and make me as white as snow. The Holy Spirit showed me that my past could be forgiven and I could start over again as a new creation. God used my friends to woo me to Himself. The Holy Spirit convinced me that Jesus is the only way to a clean conscience and a clean heart. He was the only answer for my sin. "And I will ask the Father, and He will give you another Counselor, who will never leave you. He is the Holy Spirit, who leads into all truth" (John 14:16–17 NLT). It is the Holy Spirit who allows us to see our need for a Savior, and it is the Holy Spirit who helps us to understand Scripture. The Holy Spirit will lead us into the truth of God. When I realized God would bring His Word to light and help me to understand His way for living, I knew I was not alone in my journey.

Jesus called the Holy Spirit our Counselor. A counselor is someone who guides us, leads us, and points us in the right direction. Most vehicles come with a GPS system. The destination is already known. Once we turn it on, a nice woman's voice tells us the route to take. Even though the device is usually accurate, we may still experience difficulty along the way. We never know about the weather, which can hinder us. But if we make a wrong turn, the GPS still knows where we are and can recommend alternate roads to get us back on course.

The Holy Spirit is our heavenly GPS. How well are we listening to Him? "I will bless the Lord who guides me; even at night my heart instructs me" (Ps. 16:7 NLT).

Recently a friend was going through a huge storm in her life. I was honored that she shared with me, and I immediately began to pray and ask God to equip me to minister to her. I felt helpless because I knew that she didn't need my words of comfort and encouragement but she needed God's. I asked the Holy Spirit for wisdom and guidance each time we spoke.

I called her twice a day to check on her, sent her e-mails, invited her over, and planned time to spend together so she would not have to be alone. I prayed with her and sent her Scriptures as the Holy Spirit gave them to me. I did all I could do, but my main prayer was that the Holy Spirit would minister to her, comfort her, and give her wisdom and discernment of God's will for her in her trying circumstances. Everything in me wanted to tell her to fight back, to stand up for her, to retaliate. But I knew she needed God's answer, not mine. All I could do was pray that God would tell her what to do.

The Lord gave me Psalm 37:1–6 NLT and told me He is capable of restoring any relationship.

Don't worry about the wicked. Don't envy those
who do wrong. For like grass, they soon fade
away. Like springtime flowers, they soon wither.
Trust in the Lord and do good. Then you will
live safely in the land and prosper. Take delight
in the Lord and He will give you your heart's
desires. Commit everything you do to the Lord.
Trust Him, and He will help you. He will make your
innocence as clear as the dawn, and the justice
of your cause will shine like the noonday sun.

Like my GPS, the Holy Spirit gives me direction. I have not
followed those directions perfectly at times; I have missed a
turn or two. I have even deliberately ignored His instructions.
Yet the Lord is faithful in using any situation, any wrong turn,
any time of rebellion or rejection to grow us into the image of
Christ. It is harder to get to the destination on back roads. It
will for sure take longer and we may miss out on some scenery,
but God will still guide us safely home.

Moving forward means not looking back! If all we do is stare
in the rearview mirror, we will never see the new thing God is
doing in our lives.
We are partakers in the new covenant not the old. If we are
born-again then we have the Holy Spirit as our counselor. We
have three covenant partners in one. As our covenant partner
the Holy Spirit's task is to reveal truth to us. What we do with
that truth is left up to us.

Andrew Murray, who wrote the book *The Two Covenants*,
writes,

In the Old Covenant man was given the
opportunity to prove what he could do, with

the aid of all the means of grace God could bestow. The Covenant ended in man proving his own unfaithfulness and failure. In the New Covenant, God is to prove what *He* can do with man, as unfaithful and feeble as he is, when He is allowed and trusted to do *all* the work. The Old Covenant was one dependent on man's obedience, one which he could break and did break (Jer. 31:32). The New Covenant is one which God has promised shall never be broken, for *He Himself keeps it and ensures our keeping it*. He makes it *an everlasting Covenant.*[39]

As part of the everlasting covenant we must trust that God is at work in us to make us complete in every good work to do His will. Moving forward with Christ is refreshing and renewing. God says, "Follow Me into your divine fulfillment." Jesus told us to pick up our crosses and follow Him. Once I was entangled in habitual sin. I would pray in shame, "Lord, take this away from me, for I have no strength of my own." I heard Him whisper, "Follow Me. Follow Me. Follow Me."

Leaving sin behind to follow the Good Shepherd will be one of the most freeing, exhilarating, and liberating experiences we will ever know. Scripture says that when the Holy Spirit comes he comes in power. If the Holy Spirit resides in you, you have the power to turn away from the sin that entangles and turn to God. And when we do God promised to not remember that sin. "For I will forgive their wickedness and will remember their sins no more. By calling this covenant 'new,' He has made the

---

39   Murray, 18.

first one obsolete; and what is obsolete and aging will soon disappear" (Heb. 8:12–13 NIV).

The Holy Spirit inside us calls us to obey. He calls us to desire what God desires for us. "Where the Spirit of the Lord is there is freedom" (2 Cor. 3:17 NIV). We are free to leave the prison cell that traps us. The chains that bind us have been broken; why do we put them back on when we have the key? Why do we stay in a closed, cold, dark place of shame when the door of freedom is wide open for us to walk through? "The Holy Spirit also testifies to us about this. First He says: 'This is the covenant I will make them after that time, says the Lord. I will put My laws in their hearts, and I will write them on their minds.' Then he adds: 'Their sins and lawless acts I will remember no more'" (Heb. 10:15–17 NIV).

God created the law to show humanity that the law could not be kept. After admitting to God that I was a sinner and needed Jesus as my Savior, a weight was lifted off my shoulders. As soon as we turn to Christ the Holy Spirit begins his work in us. God is committed to our spiritual growth. Sin stunts our growth. How many times in the Bible do we see God refusing to listen, to act, or to acknowledge his children because of the sin in their lives? We sin every day, and it's important to keep short accounts with God. But when we are entangled in habitual sin, God hones in on that area because it will cause us to stop growing. The longer we choose sin, the more seared our conscience can become. A seared conscience can leave us numb to the damaging effects that our sin can have on our relationship with God and those around us. Once when I was entangled in my own web of sin I realized I was paralyzed and couldn't move. The Holy Spirit led me to pray 'Jesus help me love you more!' I wanted to desperately be obedient to Christ but I realized I needed to love Him more.

"To the Jews who had believed him, Jesus said, 'If you hold to my teaching, you are really my disciples. Then you will know the truth and the truth will set you free" (John 8:31–32 NIV). Jesus links love with obedience.

The new covenant is based on love. The love of God is a motivating force.

> If you love Me, you will obey what I command ... Whoever has My commands and obeys them, he is the one who loves Me. He who loves Me will be loved by My Father, and I too will love him and show Myself to him ... If anyone loves Me, he will obey My teaching. My Father will love Him, and We will come to him and make Our home with him. He who does not love Me will not obey My teaching. These words you hear are not My own; they belong to the Father who sent Me.
>
> —John 14:15, 21, 23–24 NIV

Jesus loves us regardless of our faults and flaws. As our covenant partner He wants to see us succeed in our Christian walk and experience freedom. Scripture says that the Holy Spirit will help us to understand what God has freely given to us. Our covenant partner Jesus gives us His strength, His mind, His desires and His power to walk with Him.

Jesus does not want us to walk with Him in obedience because we are afraid of the consequences if we do not; that's not love. God's love is patient and kind. God's love is not possessive or boastful. When we operate out of love for God we don't have to strive or strain, we do so because we want to.

When we are secure in God's love for us, we are then free to love others. As His disciples, we can rest in the Spirit's power. As we do, we will be able to resist the craving of our sinful nature. In fact, Paul says, the Spirit will give us desires that are the opposite of our sinful nature. Though our daily decisions are never free from this "conflict of interest," Paul says when the Holy Spirit leads us; we are no longer subject to the law.

> But when the Holy Spirit controls our lives, he will produce this kind of fruit in us: love, joy, peace, patience, kindness, goodness, faithfulness, gentleness, and self-control. Here there is no conflict with the law. Those who belong to Christ Jesus have nailed the passions and desires of their sinful nature to his cross and crucified them there. If we are living now by the Holy Spirit, let us follow the Holy Spirit's leading in every part of our lives. Let us not become conceited, or irritate one another, or be jealous of one another.
>
> —Gal. 6:22–26 NLT

Let us not forget that nailing our sinful desires to the cross can be a daily, even minute-by-minute process. When we know we have sinned, we must take that sin to the cross immediately. We must not wait, but quickly repent and ask for forgiveness. "Who may climb the mountain of the Lord? Who may stand in His holy place? Only those whose hands and hearts are pure, who do not worship idols and never tell lies. They will receive the Lord's blessing and have right standing with God their Savior. They alone may enter God's presence and worship the God of Israel" (Ps. 24:3–6 NLT).

Repentance is the key to climbing the mountain of God. We may fall down, but through repentance, we are restored to a right relationship with our Lord.

"And in every work that he began in the service of the house of God, in the law and in the commandment, to seek his God, he did it with all his heart. So he prospered" (2 Chron. 31:21 NKJV). The key to prosperity is to follow God and serve Him with all our hearts. Many people may think prosperity is only financial, but it also means being at peace with God. Peace with God brings peace with others and a security that cannot come from anywhere or anyone else. Obedience will lead us to peace. As our covenant partner, God is committed to continually revealing His character to us according to our needs and according to His purposes. As we obey we will come to know him more and more. Yet if we continue to live year after year with the same basic knowledge of God as when we first became Christians, we can think we are living a good, moral, and pure life only to find out we are deceiving ourselves.

Hezekiah, who became king in Jerusalem when he was only twenty-five, lived in a tumultuous time when society was squeezing God out of everyday life. Kings before him did not follow the one true God. The temple had been closed. Hezekiah's first act as king was to call the priests and Levites to cleanse the temple. When the temple was ready for worship, he called the people of Judah to gather and worship again the one true God. Idolatry was popular, and worship took place in many different forms. Hezekiah destroyed the idols and tore down the heathen gods the people worshiped. He did everything in his power to serve God again and to lead his people in the same path.

Not everyone responded to the king's invitation. Some had been worshiping idols for so long that they laughed at his invitation. But others gladly returned to bring praise and worship to the one true God. The people were so deceived that they had burned incense and worshiped the brass serpent Moses had made in the wilderness. Hezekiah took this brass serpent and burned it. He then built a wall around Jerusalem for protection against its enemies and put together an army ready to defend its people. Yet it wasn't strong enough to defend itself against the Assyrian army. As Hezekiah led his people back to God, the Lord gave them favor and protection. The Assyrians were known for conquering city after city, and they marched toward Jerusalem. The king of Assyria sent a message to Hezekiah telling him his city would be destroyed and his people taken to a far country. He told Hezekiah that his God would not be able to save him. Hezekiah prayed to the Lord, and God sent an angel to kill all the Assyrian soldiers. God answered Hezekiah's prayer by giving him and the people divine protection against their relentless enemy. Before Hezekiah took over as King the people were deceived into thinking what they were doing was the right thing. As they went about living their lives they left God out. When there is no standard for truth we can easily deceive ourselves. God used Hezekiah to bring the standard of truth back into society. The standard of truth is God Himself!

Billy Graham's prayer for our nation sums up how our society has distorted its view of good and evil. He cautions against those who call good evil and evil good.

> Heavenly Father, we come before you today to ask your forgiveness and to seek your direction and guidance. We know Your Word says, "Woe to those who call evil good," but that is exactly what we have done. We have lost our spiritual equilibrium and reversed our values. We have exploited the poor and called it the lottery. We have rewarded laziness and called it welfare. We have killed our unborn and called it choice. We have shot abortionists and called it justifiable. We have neglected to discipline our children and called it building self-esteem. We have abused power and called it politics. We have coveted our neighbor's possessions and called it ambition. We have polluted the air with profanity and pornography and called it freedom of expression. We have ridiculed the time-honored values of our forefathers and called it enlightenment. Search us, oh God, and know our hearts today; cleanse us from every sin and set us free. Amen![40]

Spiritual renewal can begin with prayer. So why do I find myself using prayer as a last resort? James 5:16 NKJV says, "The effective, fervent prayer of a righteous man avails much." Can

---

40   Billy Graham, "Billy Graham's National Confession," Whole Truth Help, http://www.wholetruthhelp.com/archieves/35html, (accessed July 6, 2012).

the prayer of one person start the revival of an entire nation? It did with Moses.

After he discovered God's people worshipping the golden calf, Moses prayed that God would renew them and restore them unto Himself. His prayer was answered. How easily we, too, are drawn to worship other gods, exploit the Word of God, and turn to accepted worldly norms. As we grow in the Lord, the ways of this world should grieve our hearts until we are concerned about every soul on the path to spiritual death.

Paul prayed specifically for God's people to grow and mature in their faith. He was in prison at the time and had not been to Philippi for more than ten years, but still he took the time to pray for his fellow believers and encourage their maturity in the Lord: "And this is my prayer: that your love may abound more and more in knowledge and depth of insight, so that you may be able to discern what is best and may be pure and blameless until the day of Christ, filled with the fruit of righteousness that comes through Jesus Christ—to the glory and praise of God" (Phil. 1:9–11NIV).

Paul begins by praying that God's people will abound more and more in love through knowledge and depth of insight. The Greek word for *abound* is *peerisseuo*, meaning "to be in excess of, to exceed, to increase, or to overflow." Paul prayed that God's love would continue to grow in us and therefore overflow to others. This love is obtained though knowledge and depth of insight of who God is and how God loves. We do not naturally seek to know God's love for us. In fact the Bible says that we are not seekers at all; it's God who seeks us out.

The apostle Paul is not talking about a love based on emotions or feelings. We naturally want to be in relationships that make us happy or around people who make us laugh. But true love goes beyond happiness and feelings. The Apostle Paul is praying for us to love with a love that can come only from God Himself. This is a love not based on attraction, wealth, sense of humor, or education. It is an unconditional love.

According to *Holman Illustrated Bible Dictionary,* the Hebrew term for *love* is *chesed, which* refers to covenant love. "Jehovah is the God who remembers and keeps His covenants in spite of the treachery of people," the book says. "Biblical love has God as its object, true motivator, and source."[41]

If we look up the Greek word for *love* used in Philippians 1:9, we find it described as *agape* love. This agape love also appears in John 3:16 where God describes His love for His son and us. Agape love is a love we are capable of attaining when we have the Spirit of God residing in us. It is His constant, self-sacrificing, unconditional, active, volitional, and thoughtful love that resides in a believer. Thomas Jay Orod, a theologian, philosopher, and scholar, has defined *agape* as "an intentional response to promote well-being when responding to that which has generated ill-being."[42] In his book *The Pilgrimage*, Paulo Coelho defines *agape* as "the love that consumes,"[43] the highest and purest form of love, one that surpasses all other types of affection.

Agape love differs from other types of love. The essence of agape love is self-sacrifice. Close friendships (brotherly love)

---

41   Holman Illustrated Bible Dictionary, s.v. "Chesed".

42   Thomas Jay Orod, "Agape," Wikipedia, http://en.wikipedia.org/wiki/Agape (accessed July 7, 2012).

43   Paul Coelho, "The Pilgrimage," http://www.goodreads.com/quotes/show32900 (accessed July 7, 2012).

are described by the root word *philia*. Erotic or sensual love is described by the root word *eros*. But agape love is of God and from God. The Bible says that God is love (1 John 4:8 NIV). Love is who He is; He cannot act against His nature. Everything God does flows from His agape love. This is the love we are to pursue, Paul says. It is not a pursuit that comes naturally.

We get a picture of agape love in Corinthians. Here, in what is called the love chapter, Paul lists several characteristics of agape love.

> Love is patient, love is kind. It does not envy, it does not boast, it is not proud. It is not rude, it is not self-seeking, it is not easily angered, it keeps no record of wrongs. Love does not delight in evil but rejoices with the truth. It always protects, always trusts, always hopes, always perseveres. Love never fails.
>
> —1 Cor. 13:4–8 NIV

Ask yourself, "Am I capable of this love?" I don't think we can ever love perfectly as God loves us, but with God's help we can continue to grow in our love for Him and for others. "And hope does not disappoint us, because God has poured out his love into our hearts by the Holy Spirit, whom he has given us" (Rom. 5:5 NIV). How amazing to know that God pours His love into us. If our hope is in Christ, we will not be disappointed because God's Spirit inside of us, connected to us, will show us how to love with His kind of love. This is a love without limits or restrictions; it knows no end.

We all know actions speak louder than words. In John 13:35 NIV, Jesus said, "By this all men will know that you are My disciples, if you love one another." When we can love others with God's love, people will notice.

It is not easy to love when we have been hurt or have a good reason to be angry. Peter asked Jesus how many times we should forgive someone who has wronged us. "Up to seven times, Lord; is this enough?" he asked. Jesus told him, "Seven times seventy." In other words, there is no limit to the number of times we are to forgive our enemies. We must forgive if we are to love others with genuine love from God.

Paul said he wanted our love to abound more and more in knowledge and depth of insight. The Scriptures teach us that, if we are to abound in agape love, or if agape love is to overflow in us to others, we first need to be filled with this love. We cannot give something away that we do not have.

Jesus said, "If you are thirsty, come to Me! If you believe in Me, come and drink! For the Scriptures declare that rivers of living water will flow out from within' (When He said 'living water,' He was speaking of the Spirit, who would be given to everyone believing in Him)" (John 7:37–39 NLT).
Jesus Christ is our fountain of living water, a never-ending, limitless source of life. Once we are full of living water (Jesus), our hearts will be like a river overflowing to others. If we are full of the Spirit of God, allowing the Spirit to control us, others will experience God's love as well. If we love others with agape love, then out of this love will flow the fruit of the Spirit.

> But the fruit of the Spirit is love, joy, peace, patience, kindness, goodness, faithfulness, gentleness, and self-control. Against such

things there is no law. Those who belong to
Christ Jesus have crucified the sinful nature with
its passions and desires. Since we live by the
Spirit, let us keep in step with the Spirit. Let us not
become conceited, provoking and envying
each other.

—Gal. 5:22–26 NIV

Notice how love is the first fruit mentioned. "There are three
things that will endure—faith, hope, and love—and the
greatest of these is love" (1 Cor. 13:13 NLT). Paul prayed that
God's love would be evident in us through the power of the
Holy Spirit working in our lives. "For we are God's workmanship,
created in Christ Jesus to do good works, which God prepared
in advance for us to do" (Eph. 2:10 NIV). There is a plan for our
lives. God knows that plan. To be filled with the Spirit, we must
abide in Christ. "Yes, I am the vine; you are the branches.
Those who remain in Me, and I in them, will produce much
fruit. For apart from Me you can do nothing" (John 15:5 NLT).
We must stay connected to Jesus through the Word of God.
Jesus is the Word that became flesh. To abide in Him is to
remain in Him, to stay connected to him, to attach to Him.
The Greek word for *abide* in this passage is *meno* meaning
"to stay in a given place, state, relation or expectancy." If
we do not remain in Christ, we are capable of nothing that
matters.

If I could speak in any language in heaven or
on earth but didn't love others, I would only be
making meaningless noise like a loud gong or a
clanging cymbal. If I had the gift of prophesy,
and if I knew all the mysteries of the future and
knew everything about everything, but didn't

love others, what good would I be? And if I had the gift of faith so that I could speak to a mountain and make it move, without love I would be no good to anybody. If I gave everything I had to the poor and even sacrificed my body, I could boast about it; but if I didn't love others, I would be of no value whatsoever.

—I Cor. 13:1–4 NLT

Abiding in Christ allows us to love with His love, and through that love will come a harvest of righteous fruit to prove it. If we do not live a life of love, nothing we say will matter, nothing we know will matter, nothing we believe will matter, nothing we give will matter, nothing we accomplish will matter.

"And the most important piece of clothing you must wear is love. Love is what binds us all together in perfect harmony" (Col. 3:14 NLT). We must get up every day and put on our "God suit" so we can love others. God's love is action, not a feeling. God's love will propel us to actions that enhance His kingdom and give Him the glory He deserves.

Our love must abound in knowledge and depth of insight. What is the source of true knowledge? The Word of God gives us knowledge of who God is, what He values, how He thinks, and what is important to Him. The Greek word for *knowledge* is *epignosis,* meaning "to make one better acquainted with" or "to experience." We are to grow in our experience of God's love!

Someone once said that love experienced is love reflected. We see this in the way we love others. How we were loved as children can greatly affect how we love others. Sometimes we can be products of our environment, for better or worse. But if we will seek to know this unconditional love that God freely gives, it will help us love others the same way.

Hosea 4:6 NIV says, "My people are destroyed from lack of knowledge." The more we study God's Word the more we will be able to love with agape love. Our love should flow out of knowledge of the Word of God. We must love one another according to the right moral principles, which we learn from the Word of God.

Does this mean we are to love everybody and everything all the time? No. Real love does not turn a blind eye to the truth. According to author and pastor John MacArthur, "Biblical love seeks to know right from wrong, false from true, and seeks to make the right application of truth at the proper moments in life. It seeks to meet the needs of others and it ascertains and understands them. Love as an unregulated impulse is dangerous. But love directed by careful scrutiny and sensitive discrimination will be conformed to the truth." [44]

In other words, knowledge and discernment go together. Discernment is depth of insight into knowledge. It is applying knowledge in the right place at the right time. Discernment originates with the Holy Spirit as He leads and guides our daily lives. William Hendriksen writes: "A person who possesses love but lacks discernment may reveal a great deal of eagerness and enthusiasm. He may donate to all kinds of causes. His motives may be worthy and his intentions honorable, yet he

---

44   John MacArthur, "Essentials for Growth in Godliness Part 1," Jesus Christ Saves Ministries, http://www.jcsm.org/StudyCenter/john_macarthur/50-5.htm (accessed July 7th, 2012).

may be doing more harm than good."[45] May our love be discerning and may the Holy Spirit lead us to know true love.

The Bible says that we can speak the truth in love. If we know someone living in sin, we are not to look the other way and act as if nothing is happening. Love requires us to caution our brother about his error. We are to love the sinner but hate the sin. If we truly love our brother, we must not enable him to keep hurting himself. "My brothers, if one of you should wander from the truth and someone should bring him back, remember this: Whoever turns a sinner from the error of his way will save him from death and cover over a multitude of sins" (James 5:19–20 NIV). True love does not turn a blind eye when a brother or sister in Christ is in trouble. Love does not enable someone to self-destruct. We must love with a discerning love, doing what is right in God's eyes with the knowledge we have.
Warren Wiersbe wrote: "Truth without love is brutality, and love without truth is hypocrisy."[46] We would be hypocritical like the Pharisees if we condoned what we know is wrong in God's eyes.

Paul also prayed that believers would be able to discern what is best for them. The New Living Translation's version of Philippians 10:1 reads: "For I want you to understand what really matters." In the English Standard Version, the verse reads, "So that you may approve the things that are excellent." There is a difference between good, best, and excellent for your life. When we get down to the nitty-gritty, only God knows what

45   William Hendriksen, "Exposition Philippians (1962)," http://www. rediscoveringthebible.com/PraticalInsights.html (accessed July 7th, 2012).
46   Warren Wiersbe, "Warren Wiersbe Quotes," Goodreads Inc., http://www. goodreads.com/author/quotes/477679.warren_wiersbe. (accessed July 7, 2012).

is excellent for you. Only God knows what is perfect for you. Paul is saying, "I want you to understand what really matters!" If we pray, "Lord, teach me what really matters." Out of this alone could come life-altering decisions.

I have a good friend who has a great job with an outstanding salary, wonderful benefits, stock options, a 401(k), and perks. Yet she began to pray, "Lord, teach me what really matters." As she was sitting on the floor, playing with her children, laughing, singing, and loving them, the Lord said, "This is what matters." She told me that she knew her job was a good thing and that what she had provided for her family was beneficial, but the Lord impressed on her that she needed to spend more time with them. There was a pending promotion she was in line for at work yet at that moment she felt the Lord telling her to turn it down. Again, a discerning spirit will lead us in the best direction.

Paul asks us to pray, "Lord, show me what really matters to You! " What really matters to Him will cause us to put our selfish ambitions aside and seek His heart. Pursuing what really matters will stretch us to the limit and cause us to trust God as never before.

What really matters? We will never be where we need to be until we are with the Lord, but how great a God who will help us discern not only what is best for us, but also what is perfect! "Praise be to the name of God for ever and ever; wisdom and power are his. He changes times and seasons; He sets up kings and deposes them. He gives wisdom to the wise and knowledge to the discerning" (Dan. 2:20–21 NIV).

Andrew Murray views the knowledge of God as the very gate of heaven. In his beloved book *The Two Covenants*, he writes,

> My one great desire has been to ask Christians whether they are really seeking to find out what exactly God wants them to be and is willing to make them! It is only as they wait for "the mind of the Lord to be shown to them" that their faith can ever truly see, or accept, or enjoy what God calls "His salvation." As long as we expect God to do for us what we ask or think, we limit Him. When we believe that as high as the heavens are above the earth so His thoughts are above our thoughts, and wait on Him as *God* to do unto us *according to His Word,* as *He* means it, we shall be prepared to live the truly supernatural, heavenly life the Holy Spirit can work in us- the true Christ-life.[47]

The more we experience God's love, the more our knowledge increases in Him, the better we can determine right from wrong and discern what is best according to His plan for our lives. If we truly seek the heart of God in every decision, in everything that comes our way, the Holy Spirit will show us how to live this side of heaven. By seeking the heart of God, we will be in His will and in the secret place of peace that surpasses understanding.

In Philippians, Paul then prays that we can discern what is best, that we "may be pure and blameless until the day of Christ, filled with the fruit of righteousness that comes through

---

47   Murray, page 9..

Jesus Christ—to the glory and praise of God." The New King James Version of this verse uses the words *sincere* (pure) and *without offense* (blameless).

The word *sincerity* comes from the Latin *sine cere*, meaning *without wax*. To explain the meaning of without wax, enormous quantities of pottery came out of the Roman Empire. One could purchase pottery jars, dishes, or bowls for cooking. People who liked hosting big parties could find formal dinnerware, which was more expensive because it was more delicate and intricate. One could also find specialized pottery workshops where pottery was bought and sold. Artists could spend hundreds of hours on their work, and because inferior materials were used, the pottery might crack when fired. After investing so much time in one piece, an artisan often hid the cracks to sell the work. The artists would hide the flaws with wax to deceive the buyer. Consequently, it was important to hold a prospective purchase up to the sun so hidden damage might be revealed.

We all have cracks and flaws that we try to hide from others, but one thing is certain: when the light of God shines into a heart, it always reveals the heart's true condition. Can we walk without offense in the eyes of God when His light shines into our hearts? We may be able to fool others but none can fool God.

Most people believe they are sincere. To be sincere means to have nothing hidden. As with the clay, when we are put under pressure or in the fire, what comes out? Can we handle stress and pressure without demonstrating the qualities we hate? A sincere person is keenly aware of his faults and can openly admit them while working to mend them. One who gives excuses for his faults is using wax to cover them and deceiving him as well as others. Of course it's easier to cover up our flaws or place blame on others because that's what comes natural to us.

Don't confuse honesty with sincerity. A sincere person will keep his word but will also be sensitive to how his words affect others. The Bible says our *yes* should mean yes and our *no* mean no. A sincere person will not only hold to their word but also have a genuine concern for the well being of others.

Shopping in Hawaii with my husband, I came across an advertisement for free pearls. All I had to do was pick out an oyster and pry it open to discover if a pearl was inside. I was very excited to try, thinking I would find a pearl. I did! I was so thrilled that I wanted to put my pearl on a necklace when I got home.

When I returned home, I researched how pearls are made. To my dismay, there is a difference between a real pearl and a cultured pearl. The tiny but dramatic distinction is a minute grain of sand, along with an extended amount of time. When a tiny bit of sand finds its way into an oyster on the bottom of the sea, layers of a substance called nacre build up around the oyster to protect its tender flesh. Over the years, layer upon layer of nacre eventually creates a beautiful, genuine pearl.

A cultured pearl is formed rather quickly when man places a plastic ball inside the oyster. Again, the oyster protects itself by producing nacre around the plastic center to form a pearl. But these cultured pearls are harvested early and are prone to scratch easily due to their bogus core. The core of the pearl is not genuine, only an imitation. I realized that my five-dollar oyster probably did not contain a real pearl. A real pearl has a pure center and a genuine core. A real pearl is made by God and not by man. A real pearl can be trusted not to scratch and lose its effect.

Paul calls believers to be the real pearl. He says we are to be pure, blameless and to walk without offense. In Mark 6:42, Jesus says we can see others clearly only when our own eyes are unobstructed. To walk without offense means we must not offend others or be easily offended. If our hearts are pure before God, we will not catch ourselves questioning people's motives, finding fault, or criticizing their opinions. Instead we will look for the good in others and seek what is praiseworthy. If our hearts are pure, we will be able to see others as God sees them. In so doing, we will have grace when others offend us and be less offensive toward others. We have not arrived, but a pure heart before God will fill our lives with the fruit of righteousness that comes only through Jesus Christ. Nevertheless, our outward lives will demonstrate what is in our hearts.

chapter 7

COVENANT SECURITY

"This is the covenant I will make with them after that time," says the Lord. "I will put my laws in their hearts, and I will write them on their minds." Then he adds, "Their sins and lawless acts I will remember no more. And where these have been forgiven, there is no longer any sacrifice for sin."

—Heb. 10:16–18 NIV

A human relationship takes time to turn into something worthy of trust. To fully trust someone, we have to know him or her. Too many people have experienced a failed relationship and lost trust and confidence in another person. Trust creates a secure environment that allows us to be ourselves. Trust gives us the freedom to expose our true selves and yet have confidence we will be accepted.

God considers His people to be saints, a concept hard to grasp. You may say, "I'm not saint," but God thinks otherwise. We may not trust ourselves, but we can trust in the character of God, who says He will never forsake us, regardless of what we have done. The Sidewalk Prophets' song "You Love Me Anyway" says, "I am the thorn in your side, but you love me anyway; I am the sweat on your brow, but you love me anyway; I am the nail in your wrist, but you love me anyway; I am Judas' kiss and the man that yelled out of the crowd to shed your blood, but you love me anyway."[48] As a born-again believer God's presence is with us and in us no matter what!

The Corinthian church struggled with all kinds of ungodly behavior, yet the apostle Paul still described its members as "those who have been sanctified in Christ Jesus, saints by calling" (1 Cor. 1:2 NASB). To be sanctified means to be set apart for sacred use. Throughout Scripture, we see what God has chosen to sanctify: the Sabbath is His sanctified day; the tabernacle was His sanctified place; the Ark of the Covenant was His sanctified entity.

The moment we accept Christ as Lord and Savior, we become sanctified, set apart for His purposes. However, it wasn't that way in the Old Testament before Jesus Christ. Before Jesus' death and resurrection, God chose prophets to speak for Him, and He chose where His presence would dwell. In the Old Testament, a cloud that represented the fullness of His glory manifested God's presence. This cloud was called the *Shekinah* of God. God's presence had come to live among His people in the tabernacle (Ex. 40:34) and then later in the temple (1 Kings 8:10–11).

We see several examples in the Old Testament of God's presence residing with someone only to leave him later. God

---

48   Ben McDonald, David Frey, Mark DeLaverne, "You Love Me Anyway," Side-Walk Prophets, August 2009, Word Entertainment LLC, A Warner/ Curb Company, ASIN: B002LBSIHS.

gave the prophet Ezekiel a vision of His presence leaving the tabernacle. Because of Israel's sin, God's presence could no longer dwell among His people. God showed Ezekiel how His people were involved in idol worship. Because of their worship of other gods, the Lord said that He would deal with them in fury. He said he would neither pity nor spare them. And though they would scream for mercy, He would not listen.

Ezekiel 9 says that the glory of the God of Israel rose up from between the cherubim, where it had rested, and moved to the entrance of the temple, then over to the door. The temple was filled with a cloud of glory, and the temple courtyard glowed brightly. Finally, we see the glory of God hovering over the city and stopping above a mountain to the east. Ezekiel must have been greatly saddened to see the presence of God Himself leaving the temple and finally leaving the city.

Another example of God's presence departing is found in Judges 13. Again the Israelites had done what was evil in the Lord's sight, so He had handed them over to the Philistines, who kept them in subjugation for forty years. It is in this chapter where we read of Samson's birth to a mother unable to have children. An angel appeared and told her she would bare a son and was to never cut his hair. Her son would one day rescue Israel from the Philistines. The angel told her that her son would be dedicated to God as a Nazarite from the moment of his birth until the day of his death. What a miracle to hear from God that a barren womb would give birth to a child chosen by God to further His purposes!

The proud parents named their son Samson, which means *sunshine*. At Samson's birth, the angel of the Lord gave his parents specific instructions on how Samson was to be set apart from the world. As a Nazarite, which means one set apart or separated, Samson was never to drink wine or eat any fruit of the vine. He could not touch a dead body, whether animal or human, and he was to never cut his beautiful, thick hair.

The Lord blessed the child as he grew to be a very strong man. We read of Samson ripping apart a lion's jaws, snapping rope from his arms as if it were string, and killing thousands of men with the jawbone of a donkey. It was obvious that Samson had supernatural strength. His strength came from the Lord, who worked through him to accomplish what God wanted for His people.

Leave it to a manipulating woman to uncover his secret vow and cut his hair for money! Delilah convinced Samson to tell her where his strength came from. One of the most heart-wrenching verses in the Old Testament is Judges 16:20. After Samson broke his vow to God as a Nazarite, he did not realize the Lord had left him. The strength he had always relied on, the strength of the Lord, had vanished once his hair was cut. The Philistines then captured Samson, gouged out his eyes, bound him with bronze chains, and made him grind grain in prison. The man whose name meant *sunshine* never saw the sun again.

During a great celebration, the Philistines wanted to make a spectacle of Sampson. They brought him out of prison to perform like a puppet for them. Samson asked the servant who was leading him to place his hands against the two pillars supporting the temple. The temple was crowded with people; the roof held around three thousand people. Samson then asked the Lord to remember him and renew his strength one more time so he could pay back the Philistines for the loss of his eyes. The Lord answered his prayer. Samson put his hands on the center pillars and pushed with all his might. The temple crashed down on the Philistines. Scripture says that Samson killed more people that day than he had previously during his entire life.

Samson's life was cut short. A life given a divine purpose by the Lord ended in humiliation and sorrow. Samson chose to compromise with the world. He did not set himself apart from the things of this world that would pull him away from his God. God's presence left him, and he did not even know it until it was too late. Samson's choices left him alone and stranded. He dishonored his parents, deserted his promises as a Nazarite, and disobeyed his God. Samson was physically blind, but the sin in his life had already blinded him from not choosing the path of God. The power in Samson's life was gone. His supernatural strength left him, and he became vulnerable to the attack of the enemy.

As Christians, we are called by God to be set apart, different, separated from this world in thought, word, and deed. Samson's first mistake was being unequally yoked with Delilah. He loved Delilah, but we know she did not share this love for him. She knew she had him under her spell and would destroy him. Isn't that what sin does to our families, our children, and us? The longer we allow it to remain in our lives the more it destroys. Samson gave away everything he valued in the name of love. He compromised his calling, and God eventually let him go. How sad a story when there was so much potential in this one man who was meant to shine light in areas that had been dark for so long.

When I think of Samson, my heart sinks because I can relate to him. I, too, have chosen the way of this world rather what I know to be right in the eyes of God. But just as Jesus knows our true potential, He also knows and identifies with our weaknesses. Samson's strength left him because God left him. But as partners under the new covenant, we walk according to the Spirit of God with our covenant partner's strength. "He has made us competent as ministers of a new covenant—-not of the letter but of the Spirit; for the letter kills, but the Spirit gives life" (2 Cor. 3:6 NIV).

Kay Arthur writes,

> The gift of the Holy Spirit given under the New Covenant is the guarantee of our inheritance, our sharing in covenant oneness all that belongs to our Covenant God and Savior. He is the pledge of our redemption and the guarantee of a new body—an eternal "house." We have the certain and sure hope of heaven, of eternal life.
> The Old Covenant exposed our sin and our need. The New Covenant provides the solution: the Holy Spirit.
> The Old Covenant enlightened.
> The New Covenant empowers.
> The Old Covenant revealed our sin.
> The New Covenant releases us from sin's power.[49]

I have heard it said that there is only one thing greater than having a relationship with God, and that's knowing you have a relationship with God. As born-again Christians, we should know that our relationship with God through Jesus Christ is

---

49   Arthur, page 266.

eternal. God doesn't change His mind about our salvation. To speak of covenant security, we must assume that we are talking about a born-again Christian, a person who has invited Jesus Christ to live in his heart and surrendered his life to his new king.

According to a recent survey, 84 percent of Americans call themselves Christians. If these 84% died and stood before Jesus and were asked why He should allow them to enter the kingdom of heaven, do you think all of them would have the same answer? Some might say, "I should enter because I prayed a prayer in Sunday school," or "because I was baptized," or "because I gave money to support the church." Still others might say, "I should enter because I read Your Word and served You faithfully. I'm a religious person; I believe in God, and went to church every Sunday." All these answers are good gestures but the only hope we have is in Jesus.

"And this is what God has testified: He has given us eternal life, and this life is in His Son. So whoever has God's Son has life; whoever does not have His Son does not have life" (1 John 5:11–12 NLT).

If it were left to us to make the right choices to get into heaven, then no one would be there! All of us live the life of Samson. But if we are born again, our security in God's presence within us cannot be taken away. Hebrews 13:5 NIV says that God will never leave us or forsake us. A born-again Christian's confidence and security of salvation rest in Jesus Christ alone.

Our eternal security depends on what God has done for us, not on what we have done for God. How presumptuous to assume that there is anything we can do for God! If salvation rests upon what we do or do not do, then salvation is about us, not about Christ. If our good works can get us into heaven, Jesus would say, "Good job. You made it." Salvation cannot be viewed as a goal we achieve or a prize we win. It has nothing to do with us. The only part we have in salvation is accepting or rejecting the Son of God. If we accept Jesus as our Savior, God does not change His mind about our eternal destiny. We know that this security is not a license to sin, but a promise that connects us with our Creator forever.

A Pharisee in the Bible named Nicodemus wanted to talk to Jesus late one night. This was odd because a Pharisee was considered a religious leader who taught the people a strict interpretation of the law. The Pharisees were actually threatened by Jesus because his words opposed the law. Jesus went as far as calling the Pharisees hypocrites. Nicodemus must have known that Jesus often challenged the Pharisees' authority and views of the Scriptures.

But there was something different about Nicodemus. When he addressed Jesus, he called him *teacher*. Did he want to learn from Jesus? Was his heart open to what Jesus had to say? He came to Jesus after dark so other Pharisees would not see him. Nicodemus took it upon himself to seek truth. He believed in God, but did not yet believe Jesus was the Messiah.

He said to Jesus, "Teacher, we all know that God has sent You to teach us." Many today believe Jesus was merely a good teacher and had wise things to say. Nicodemus said it was obvious that God was with Jesus because of all the miracles He had performed. Jesus replied that unless Nicodemus was born again, he could never see the kingdom of heaven. Perplexed, Nicodemus asked how he could fit back into his mother's womb and be born again. Jesus replied, "The truth is, no one can enter the Kingdom of God without being born again of water and Spirit. Humans can reproduce only human life, but the Holy Spirit gives new life from heaven" (John 3:5–6 NLT).

Spirit is the English translation for the Greek word *pneuma*. In Hebrew, the word is *ruah*. Both mean *spirit* and *wind*; there is a double meaning. Jesus said, "Just as you can hear the wind but can't tell where it comes from or where it is going, so you can't explain how people are born of the Spirit" (John 3:8 NLT). Jesus was comparing the Holy Spirit to the wind. We cannot see where the wind is coming from or going; we can only feel it. We cannot explain how others are born again, but we can see changes in their lives.

As a Pharisee, Nicodemus was a member of the Jewish council called the Sanhedrin. This group of men had discussed ways to kill Jesus. After Nicodemus' encounter with Jesus, the only other time we hear of him is when he joined Joseph of Arimathea in asking for Jesus' body to provide for His burial. In doing so, Nicodemus knew that he was risking his life. Here we see a changed man, a man who questioned everything and sought truth. In the end, we see a man who proved his spiritual rebirth with the risk he took.

Jesus said that flesh gives birth to flesh and the spirit gives birth to the spirit. We cannot control when we are physically born, nor can we control when we are spiritually reborn. God calls all people to Himself. "For God so loved the world that He gave His only begotten Son that whoever believes in Him shall not perish but have eternal life" (John 3:16 NKJV). This new life, this rebirth, is received through faith in Jesus

Christ. There is a difference in knowing God and believing God. Nicodemus knew Jesus, but he did not believe until he sought for himself who Jesus was. We know Nicodemus believed, because who would risk his life for something he did not believe in?

How do you know that you know Jesus? Have you invited Jesus to come into your life? Do you believe He is the only begotten Son of God who died on the cross for the forgiveness of your sins? The Bible says all who call upon the name of the Lord will be saved. If you want Jesus in your life, if you want to be reborn and become a new creation, pray this prayer in the sincerity of your heart: "Lord Jesus, I admit that I am a sinner and I ask You into my life. I ask that the Holy Spirit take up residence within me. I believe You are the only Son of God who died for the forgiveness for my sins. I thank you, Jesus, for this new life you have given me."

As believers, we should have a desire within us to please our Lord. If we are truly born again, we will want to obey Jesus. "We know that we have come to know Him if we obey His commands. The man who says, 'I know Him,' but does not do what He commands is a liar, and the truth is not in him. But if anyone obeys His word, God's love is truly made complete in him. This is how we know we are in Him: Whoever claims to live in Him must walk as Jesus did" (1 John 2:3–6 NIV).

Jesus said if we love Him, we would obey Him. He did not say if we obey Him that means we love Him. Do we have a desire to live holy lives, to follow God's ways, and become who Jesus intended us to be? Do we want to be closer to God? Are we sensitive to the sin in our lives? Do we talk with Jesus, listen to what He is telling us to do, and then obey out of love for Him?

These questions are desires God gives his people. God-given desires placed in a new heart of flesh.

When we are born again, we are adopted into the family of God. Other believers become our brothers and sisters, not just other people, because we are connected to them spiritually.

Do we have a desire to be around other believers? Do we desire to treat others, as we want to be treated? Do we want to love others and forgive others the way Christ loves and forgives us? Do we want to tell people of the great things God has done for us, what He is teaching us, how He is growing us? Do we give glory to God for all that is in our lives? Are we connected with a body of believers? Do we attend a church where we can be spiritually fed from God's Word? Do we want to see others the way God sees them? "We know we have passed from death to life, because we love our brothers. Anyone who does not love remains in death. Anyone who hates his brother is a murderer, and you know that no murderer has eternal life in him" (1 John 3:14–15 NIV).

Is your life producing fruit? Jesus said that a good tree produces good fruit and a bad tree produces bad fruit. "No one who lives in Him keeps on sinning. No one who continues to sin has either seen Him or known Him" (I John 3:6 NIV). This doesn't mean that if we sin we do not know God. Rather, one who is truly born again cannot keep sinning and be unaware of what he is doing. The Holy Spirit inside of us will let us know that we are out of God's will. A born-again believer will have a desire to stop sinning, break free, and be delivered. We can choose to ignore Him, but our covenant partner will remind us that we are His children and that He wants us to be holy. "To the Jews who had believed Him, Jesus said, 'If you hold to My teaching, you are really My disciples. Then you will know the truth, and the truth will set you free'" (John 8:31–32 NIV).

Jesus is the only way to God. When we accept this truth, He forms an everlasting covenant with us. "For by grace you have been saved through faith and that not of yourselves; it is a gift of God, not of works, lest anyone should boast" (Eph. 2:8–9 NKJV). To believe in someone is to trust him. We cannot put our faith and trust in a religion, a church membership, or ourselves. Only in the Lord Jesus Christ can we place our faith, hope, and trust. "And this is what God has testified: He has given us eternal life, and this life is in his Son. So whoever has God's Son has life; whoever does not have His Son does not have life" (1 John 5:11–12 NLT).

In John 14:6 NIV, Jesus said, "I am the way and the truth and the life. No one comes to the Father except through Me."

Jesus said in John 10:9 NKJV, "I am the door. If anyone enters by Me, he will be saved, and will go in and out and find pasture."

John 3:36 NKJV says, "He who believes in the Son has everlasting life; and he who does not believe in the Son shall not see life, but the wrath of God abides on him."

In the Bible, Jesus is often called the Good Shepherd. A shepherd is responsible for his sheep. David, as a shepherd, made sure his sheep had food and water. He checked them for disease, helped the pregnant ones have their babies, and kept them safe. David led the sheep to good pastures, taught them to stay together, and went after any that strayed.

Shepherds would bring their flock home to the fold at night. A sheepfold was a circular wall about ten feet high with a single opening that served as a door. Nothing could get in or out without passing the shepherd. The shepherd had to be willing to tackle wolves, lions, or bears that might come in the middle of the night to devour the sheep. He had to be willing to risk his life to protect his flock. He would lie in front of the gate to protect the sheep from predators trying to enter the sheepfold.

> I assure you, anyone who sneaks over the wall of a sheepfold, rather than going through the gate, must surely be a thief and a robber! For a shepherd enters through the gate. The gatekeeper opens the gate for him, and the sheep hear his voice and come to him. He calls his own sheep by name and leads them out. After he has gathered his own flock, he walks ahead of them and they follow him because they recognize his voice. They won't follow a stranger; they will run from him because they don't recognize his voice.
>
> —John 10:1–5 NLT

Jesus explained that He is the Good Shepherd who lay down His life for His sheep. As a shepherd knows his sheep, Jesus knows you and me. He knows how many hairs are on our heads; He knows the words we are going to say before they come out of our mouths. He weighs the motives of our hearts and sees us for who we really are. He sees all our insecurities, mistakes, and messes. When we stray, we can turn back to God and hear Him saying, "Follow Me. Follow Me."

Jesus says, "I am the good shepherd; I know My sheep and My sheep *know Me*—just as the Father knows Me, I know the Father—and I lay down My life for the sheep" (John 10:14–15 NIV). The Greek root words for know is *ginosko,* meaning to know experientially. We know because we have experienced. People cannot fully understand something they have not experienced. In the Bible, the word *know* carries an intimate meaning: "Cain knew his wife and she bore a son." This implies a deep love relationship.

The more we experience God, the better we know His character. Jesus said His sheep, His children, have experienced what it is like to hear His voice, to be comforted by His presence, and to walk in His peace. Jesus' relationship with His children is not about religion or doctrine, nor is it even spiritual. It is personal. Jesus has millions of sheep, but knows each one personally.

Jesus said He came to seek and to save those who are lost. When a shepherd lost one sheep, he left the whole flock to diligently seek out the one that got away. Finding the animal, he threw a party. How often we are like the sheep that tries to enter everywhere but through the gate that seems to have lost its way.

Is God seeking after you? Listen to His voice. Respond to His call. Continue to follow His leading. His sheep know Him, but He knows His sheep even more. Jesus knows us better than we know ourselves, and He loves us.

CLOSING
REMEMBER THE RAINBOW

In the Old Testament, Noah trusted God's plan for him and for his sons and their wives. People thought he was crazy. Noah was building an ark when no cloud was in the sky. But Noah was in constant communication with God, abiding in His presence, and knew of God's plan to flood the earth.

The first account of covenant in the Bible is the covenant God made with Noah. Noah's ark was four hundred fifty feet long. He was six hundred years old when the flood came. Noah did everything God told him to do, from applying the exact specifications for the ark to handpicking each animal and its mate. Then the floodgates were opened and it rained for forty days and forty nights. Water covered the mountaintops. And it took one hundred and fifty days for the water to recede after the rain stopped.

Once Noah, his family, and the animals were locked in the ark, there was no turning back. God closed the door. No one could enter the boat.

When Noah and his family finally emerged from the ark, God blessed them and gave them a sign that He would never flood the earth again. God made a promise that He would never again do what He had just done.

> When I send clouds over the earth, the rainbow will be seen in the clouds, and I will remember my covenant with you and with everything that lives. Never again will there be a flood that will destroy all life.
>
> —Genesis 9:14-15 NLT

When God says, "Never again," he means never again! Noah trusted God with his son's life and his own completely. After this flood Noah had just rode out the storm of his life. Stepping out of the arc for the first time standing on dry land he looked up to see a rainbow. He was one of eight people on earth and he began his new life by worshiping God. The first thing he did was fall to his knees praise God for His faithfulness.

The sign of God's promise was a rainbow, which speaks of second chances. When we are faithless, when we fall to temptation, when we disappoint God, He remains faithful. We need to start looking for rainbows in our life. God's promises never fail when we do. We can go back to his promises and start over again. God promises that sin will *never again* reign over us (Rom. 8:9-11 NLT). God promises that we *never again* need to be afraid (John 14:27 NLT). God promises that we *never again* need to worry about the future for His peace will guard our hearts and minds (Phil. 4:7 NLT). We need to *never again* be ignorant of his will, because his word is a "lamp" and a "light" to our path (Ps. 119:105 NLT). *Never again* do we need to live as defeated Christians (Rom. 8:37 NLT).

After the wind and the rain are gone and the sun comes out the rainbow will remind us that we live securely under the covenant of God.

When we are in the hand of God, nothing can snatch us away from Him. We are in an ark of security. His grip on us is eternal. We can venture that God has a double grip on His children: If we are in the hands of Jesus, we are in the hands of the Father. Who or what could pull us away from Him?

Charles Spurgeon comments on the security of covenant,

> Elohim, as the Creator and Preserver, takes care of living things to preserve them; but the Lord, even Jehovah, the covenanting God, interposes in great mercy to protect His chosen servant. It was Jehovah Who entered into solemn league and covenant with His servant Noah that He would preserve him in the ark, and float him into the new world in it; and as Jehovah the covenanting One He shut him in. There is no security like that, which was given us by the covenant grace. The hand, which was lifted to swear our safety, has also been outstretched to affect it. The everlasting covenant ordered in all things and sure guarantees salvation to all who represented by the Great Head and Surety of that covenant, even our Lord Jesus. Love and power cooperate with faithfulness and truth to keep the chosen from all danger. Dwell much upon the Covenant, and note the immutable pledges by which it is secured and the immortal principles upon which it is found. Try to suck out the delicious sweetness which is to be found

in the hive of the Covenant; for if you are an advanced child of God no form of truth can be more nourishing or refreshing to your mind.[50]

We see our covenant partner's role in keeping us secure in Him. What is our part as Jesus' covenant partner? Is there nothing we can give back, nothing we can do but rest in His assurance? Yes, we can rest assured that our salvation is secure, but because God calls His people to action—to find where He is calling them—we cannot sit idle. Our part is to put our faith into action.

In Mark 12:29–30 NLT, a Pharisee asks Jesus which commandment is the most important. Jesus replies, "The most important commandment is this: 'Hear, O Israel! The Lord our God is the one and only Lord. And you must love the Lord your God with all your heart, all your soul, your entire mind, and all your strength."

Jesus tells us to love the Lord with everything we've got—heart (emotions), soul (will), mind (choices), and strength (physical being). Love Him and receive the blessing of the covenant!

---

50   Charles H. Spurgeon, "The Treasury of David," Phillip R. Johnson, http://
        www.spurgeon.org/treasury/ps096.htm (accessed July 7, 2012).

CPSIA information can be obtained at www.ICGtesting.com
Printed in the USA
LVOW130321160113

315847LV00003B/11/P